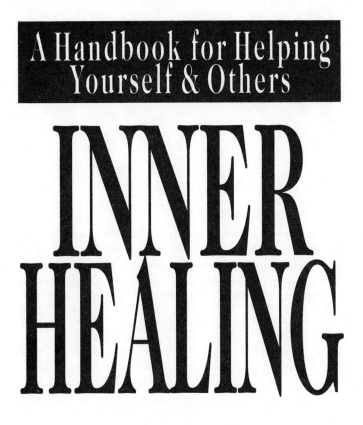

A Handbook for Helping
Yourself & Others

INNER HEALING

Mike Flynn
& Doug Gregg

INTERVARSITY PRESS
DOWNERS GROVE, ILLINOIS 60515

InterVarsity Press® is the book-publishing division of InterVarsity Christian Fellowship®, a student movement active on campus at hundreds of universities, colleges and schools of nursing in the United States of America, and a member movement of the International Fellowship of Evangelical Students. For information about local and regional activities, write Public Relations Dept., InterVarsity Christian Fellowship, 6400 Schroeder Rd., P.O. Box 7895, Madison, WI 53707-7895.

Cover illustration: Roberta Polfus

ISBN 0-8308-1664-X

Printed in the United States of America ♾

Library of Congress Cataloging-in-Publication Data

Flynn, Mike, 1940-
    Inner healing: a handbook for helping yourself & others/Mike
Flynn & Doug Gregg.
        p.   cm.
    Includes bibliographical references.
    ISBN 0-8308-1664-X (alk. paper)
    1. Spiritual healing.   I. Gregg, Douglas H.   II. Title.
BT732.5.F555   1993
234'.13—dc20   93-41897
                                                                    CIP

17	16	15	14	13	12	11	10	9	8	7	6	5
07	06	05	04	03	02	01						

*We gratefully dedicate this book
to the hundreds of students,
parishioners, conferees and friends
who have enabled us to grow
in the work of the Holy Spirit by allowing us
to pray with them.*

1

WHAT IS THE MINISTRY OF INNER HEALING?

One *Sunday I (Mike) was depressed all morning. I'm a pastor, but* conducting that day's church services did nothing to alleviate the depression. Rather dully, I decided after lunch to take a nap. I was trying to escape from depression into sleep, but I tossed about on the bed and couldn't fall asleep.

Finally, in irritation, I thought of the Lord Jesus and asked, "What's this all about, anyway?" Immediately I remembered a scene from my college years. I had been president of the Interfaith Council, and we had sponsored a physicist who spoke in one of the dorm lounges on "banning the bomb." Afterward a semicircle of four or five of us were chatting with him, and he asked me a simple question.

All of a sudden my mind went blank. I knew the question was simple, but I could not think of the answer. I stood there in increasing embarrassment as he and my fellow students stared at me, awaiting my answer.

When it finally occurred to him that my silence was terminal, he sup-
plied the answer himself and continued the conversation.

I was devastated. From that moment on, I was convinced that I was
not intelligent. I can even remember times of study when I suddenly
pushed back from my desk, refusing to spend any more time studying:
"I'm stupid, so what's the use?"

Now, lying on my bed that Sunday afternoon, I asked Jesus to enter
into that scene, put his arms about that young man who was me, comfort
me, take embarrassment away and replace it with healing, acceptance
and assurance. At the end of the prayer, as if from a great distance there
came nearer and nearer a single word which was finally resounding in
my ears. It was the word *worthy*. Worthy! Worthy! Worthy!

I had felt unworthy because of my belief that I had an inferior intellect. I have since realized that, even were that true, that is no reason for
self-rejection. But that's where I was at the time, and Jesus graciously
came to me at the point of my need and healed me. I rose from that
bed with an enhanced appreciation for my intellect as well as complete
freedom from depression. From that moment on, the memory of that
embarrassing moment from my college days has caused me no pain.
Rather, it is an occasion of deep joy because it reminds me of Jesus' love
and acceptance of me and of his eagerness to heal me of life's hurts.

*   *   *

For several minutes I (Doug) had been praying with a small group
of others for Cynthia regarding allergies, medical problems and anxiety—especially anxiety about her health. Not much was happening, and
we were preparing to close, as I asked the Lord one more time, under
my breath, "Jesus, what are you doing? How are *you* praying for Cynthia?"

Immediately I saw, in my imagination, a word in the distance. It was
a long word and began with the letter *M,* but I could not read it. It was
like trying to read the smallest line on the eye doctor's chart. And the
word wasn't getting any closer. "What is that, Lord?" I asked. And I heard

the word *mendacity*. I knew I'd heard that word before, but for the life of me I could not remember what it meant. During a pause in our prayers I asked, "Does anyone know what the word *mendacity* means?"

No one did, but Cynthia hopped up, got her dictionary and looked up the word. "It means 'the quality of being mendacious,' and that means being 'false or untrue.' "

"Oh no," I thought, squirming in my seat. "That can't be right." We all knew Cynthia to be a person of honesty and integrity.

We all stared at the floor, slightly embarrassed, until someone said, "Is it possible that you have been living a lie from the enemy, that you are believing something that's not true?"

Tears formed in Cynthia's eyes. "I think you may be right," she said. "When I was born, my mother couldn't breast-feed me, and I was allergic to cow's milk. I would throw up and be sick, and it took a long time for them to figure out what I could digest. Ever since I can remember I have been fearful and anxious about what I eat, because I am afraid I will die if I eat the wrong thing."

We continued to talk together about Cynthia's early childhood. And we talked about what it means to trust in Jesus and to know that as believers we are eternally secure in him because he has won the victory over death. Verses from Scripture—Hebrews 2:14-15—came to Cynthia's mind, and we looked them up and read: "Since the children have flesh and blood, he too shared in their humanity so that by his death he might destroy him who holds the power of death—that is, the devil—and free those who all their lives were held in slavery by their fear of death."

As we returned to prayer, Cynthia asked God to forgive her for not trusting him with her life and to heal her of anxiety and fear of death. At this point Jesus took charge, showing Cynthia that he had been present with her in her mother's womb, surrounding her with his love and peace. He made her, knew everything about her, shared in her pain and was ready to take the hurt and fear into himself. She was reminded that she had been alone in an incubator for several weeks just after birth, but she realized that Jesus had been there with her, protecting her, ensuring her life—one of the group saw his angels surrounding the incubator. Jesus showed her that he had been taking care of her in those first years of life. And finally, she saw Jesus put "a spirit of death" into a locked trunk and throw away the key.

Through people's care, through prayer and through Scripture, Jesus reached through a lifelong habit of fear to bring healing to Cynthia.

*   *   *

Jonathan was in his early thirties. I (Mike) had met him at a conference and agreed to see him when he came through town on his way to Europe to take up the directorship of a Christian ministry. He mentioned several areas of emotional need, and I prayed for them.

Then, in a moment of stillness, two impressions superimposed themselves in my thinking. One was the memory of a vacant lot a couple blocks from the home where I lived as a child. Dump trucks had deposited a dozen loads of topsoil, which provided a wonderful battlefield on which the neighborhood boys played army. The other impression was of a burned-out army tank.

I recognized that the Lord was leading me to pray for an issue that neither Jonathan nor I had mentioned to that point in our session. My prayer went something like this:

Lord Jesus, I now ask you to move to the time when Jonathan was about twelve years of age. I envision a scene in which the two of you are playing army in a burned-out tank. [Suddenly Jonathan involuntarily gasps.] You two are the best of friends, and you spend a whole Saturday doing nothing but playing army together in this tank. One of you is the driver for a while, and the other is manning the howitzer. Then you change positions.

Having played together all morning, the two of you sit on the floor of the tank and share your lunches. You're laughing. You're telling jokes. And you're thoroughly enjoying each other's company. [Jonathan is weeping audibly now.] After lunch, Lord, the two of you make up a couple more battles which you pretend to fight, full of heroism and bravery and camaraderie. You just have the most wonderful time together.

Finally, when you have to go to your homes for dinner, you part full of the gladness of friendship and good times together.

After a moment of silence, Jonathan looked up through tear-washed eyes and said, "How did you know about the tank?"

"What do you mean?" I asked.

"I was an army brat. I forgot to tell you that earlier. We were always moving from one base to another. Being somewhat shy, I had trouble making new friends. And whenever I did make a friend, I had to leave him the next time we moved, which was always too soon. So my childhood was miserable. One day I found an old burned-out tank on the base. I climbed in and spent the whole day weeping over my lack of friends and trying to comfort myself. So when you started praying about that very need—in a burned-out tank!—I knew that Jesus had been aware of my pain and that he was healing it."

As I listened to him, tears began to stream down *my* cheeks. What a wonderful Lord! What a gracious healer! What a blessed Savior! As I considered what Jesus had done for this man, I knew that he was going to have fewer problems with relationships in the ministry on which he was embarking, for he had long struggled with a fear that no one really liked him. Jesus had squarely addressed a painful memory that lay at the root of that fear.

* * *

"I hate him!" she exclaimed, with a forcefulness which shocked us. Laura, an eighteen-year-old college student, had asked a small team, led by me, Doug, to pray for her. As we interviewed her, it came out that she had rejected her father early in life because of physical and emotional abuse—being verbally abused and slapped hard on the face and bottom for not living up to what seemed unfair and unrealistic expectations.

Laura went on to explain that she had felt unwanted, rejected and unloved and had become rebellious. In high school, especially during her junior year when she lost her two best friends, Laura tried to find ways to be loved and to love herself. It was during this period that masturbation became a compulsive habit. In college, as she grew in her relationship to Christ, Laura felt more and more shame and humiliation about the compulsive masturbation.

The team now felt that we had enough data to begin some informed prayer, which we began by simply asking, "Father, would you give Laura a memory of something she experienced which you want to heal at this time?" We kept silence for a couple of minutes.

Then Laura said, "I remember coming home from high school one day when I was lonely and depressed. I plopped down in front of the TV in the family room and—uh, well—masturbated."

"How did that make you feel?"

"I felt ashamed, humiliated and defeated."

"If Jesus could be present with you in that scene, would you allow him to be there?"

"I don't think he'd want to be there," she answered.

"Well, he called himself the friend of sinners. Why don't you allow him into your sin?" We spoke for several moments from the Scriptures about Jesus' compassion and mercy.

Finally Laura said, "OK."

"Then just let him be there in the family room with you," we said.

After a couple of minutes, Laura surprised the team by exclaiming, "He's beside me and he's not angry!" As tears of relief began to flow down her cheeks, she continued, "He knows what I'm doing, but he's not angry. He's saying, 'This isn't good for you, Laura. I know you want to fill your lonely need for love, but you can't do it this way. I am the one who can fill the empty places in your heart.' "

One of the team had the same impression as she, adding that Jesus also seemed to be saying, "You know, Laura, I don't like TV that much. It's not very good for you. I'm here because I want to be with you." Laura began to receive the truth of God's love and care; her shame was broken; she repented of her sexual behavior; she forgave her father for his abuse; and she made positive steps toward self-acceptance.

Laura's emotional healing was prompted by Jesus' ability and willingness to enter her pain but not share her sense of shame, embarrassment and humiliation about herself. His straightforward willingness to be with her, even in sin, enabled her to receive his equally straightforward confrontation of illicit behavior and be relieved of its underlying causes.

What Is It?

What are we to make of the "inner healing" that these stories describe?[1] Is inner healing just psyching people out of their emotional pain? Is it nothing more than the effects of an act of human kindness and sensitivity? Is it a form of bogus spirituality? Or is it a genuine act of God? If so, how does it work? Why does it work? Does it always work? Is it overused? Can it be misused? What's the difference between inner healing and therapy? If inner healing is valid, why don't we see the words *inner healing* in the Bible? What is the theological basis for ministering in this way? Most important of all, is it of God? And if it is, how can we keep it in God?

These are the questions we will address throughout this book. In this chapter let's begin by clarifying what inner healing is and what it is not.

Inner healing is release. Over the space of a dozen years, my wife, Sue, and I (Mike) had three healthy boys and three miscarriages. Two or three weeks after the third miscarriage, Sue was feeling discouraged and frightened that she would be unable to carry another pregnancy to term; yet we both wanted one more child. Divided between fear and desire, she found herself immobilized and depressed.

One afternoon I sat down beside her on the couch and took her hand. After talking about the miscarriage for a few minutes, I suggested that we pray. "Lord Jesus," I said, "please go back a couple of weeks ago to be with Sue in the hospital, when she learned that she was losing the baby. Please reach into her heart somehow and take away the fear and the pain and the disappointment. Heal her of these hurts,

Lord, and give her your peace. Amen."

A few days later Sue approached me saying, "Guess what!"

"What?" I replied.

"It doesn't hurt anymore."

I'm not too swift on the uptake sometimes, so I said, "*What* doesn't hurt?"

Pursing her lips and narrowing her eyes in frustration at my dullness, she said, "It doesn't hurt to remember the miscarriage!" And about ten months later we had our fourth and last—and healthy—baby boy, Joel.

What does this example tell us about inner healing? That inner healing is *release*. Sue was released from her pain, from the immobilizing aspects of her disappointment, and from her fear.

Inner healing is correction. Several studies with twins and other siblings have shown that in cases where two children were mistreated equally by their parents, one may emerge from childhood with severe emotional abnormalities while the other is relatively normal. The best evidence seems to be that the *response* of the children to the abuse is a significant determinant of the *results* of the abuse. A child who responds with anger and resentment seems to end up emotionally sick or hurt, whereas a child who responds with forgiveness, understanding or some other dismissal of the abusive behavior emerges healthy.[2] Inner healing encourages those who have been hurt to utilize biblical and spiritual insights to correct their response to the abuse. Thus inner healing is a correction.

You may be thinking, "Wait a minute! It's not the *kid's* fault that he was abused. Why does *he* have to be corrected?"

You are right: the abuse is not the child's fault. But consider what Jesus said: "And if anyone causes one of these little ones who believe in me to sin, it would be better for him to be thrown into the sea with a large millstone tied around his neck" (Mk 9:42). In other words, there are degrees of sin. There is the greater sin of the person who causes a little one to sin, but there is also the lesser sin of the little one.

All sin, major and minor, needs repentance and forgiveness, even if the sin was prompted by someone's abuse. If we correct our sin of resentment toward those who hurt us, Jesus has a remarkable way of removing the emotional effects of that hurt.

Some children learn this early in life. Many of us, however, do not understand forgiveness until we are adults.

Inner healing may also be a reframing of a past event. Reframing is a way of gaining a new perspective on something that happened in the past.

Once I was praying for a young woman whose emotional growth was blocked by her anger over her father's lack of affection.

"Did he beat you?" I asked.

"Oh no! He never did that."

"Did he overcorrect you?"

"No, he didn't do that either."

"Well, what did he do that hurt you?"

"It's not what he did but what he didn't do," she replied. "He didn't hug me and tell me he loved me."

"Hmmm," I thought. Then an idea came to me, and I prayed, "Lord Jesus, I ask you to show Ginny a picture of her father's childhood."

After a few seconds, there was a soft gasp and then tears. As though her father were present, she began to address him: "Oh Daddy, I'm so sorry! I knew in my head that your mother died when you were six, but I never imagined that you hugged yourself in pain in the corner of your room, longing for her touch. I never realized you were so bruised by her absence."

In those few minutes Ginny gained a new perspective on her father's aloofness. She realized that he simply couldn't come out of his own pain enough to affirm his affection for her directly, so he had done it indirectly through making a living for his family and protecting, housing, feeding, clothing and educating them.

Notice that nothing in Ginny's past was changed except her perspective on it. In this case, that was enough.

Inner healing is exchange. Often in the ministry of inner healing I have felt led to ask Jesus to remove the negative effects of a past event and replace them with positive ones. The prayer is not that the event itself be changed, but the results of the event. For example, I might ask Jesus to take rejection out of someone's heart and replace it with his acceptance. Or I might ask him to remove guilt and replace it with the joy of salvation.

In this way, inner healing is exchange. It is acting on the central dynamic of the saving work of Christ. In 2 Corinthians 5:21 Paul states, "God made him who had no sin to be sin for us, so that in him we might become the righteousness of God." Righteousness for sin: that is a magnificent exchange! And 1 Peter 2:24 reiterates this concept: "He himself bore our sins in his body on the tree, so that we might die to sins and live for righteousness; by his wounds you have been healed."

Matthew quotes Isaiah's prediction that Jesus would extend the dynamic of exchange to burdens other than sin: "He took up our infirmities and carried our diseases" (Mt 8:17; see Is 53:4). In inner healing, Jesus and the needy person enter into an exchange. Jesus says, "Because of my love for you, I don't want the hurtful things of the past to determine the present condition of your self-image, attitudes, feelings or behaviors. So I will take those negative factors from you and replace them with the good things of God. Just as you released your sin to me when you accepted me as your Savior, so you can also release to me your hurts, fears, shames, angers, lusts and lacks. In exchange for them I will give you my healing, assurance, forgiveness, acceptance and identity."

Inner healing is usually a process more than an event. Memories tend to arrange themselves in layers, like the layers of an onion. Just as an outer layer of an onion must be peeled away before the next one can be reached, so also memories usually have to be addressed in some ordered sequence, with one level of healing giving rise to another.

Sometimes the arrangement of the sequence is crucial. Just as you have to open a cupboard before you can take something out of it, you have to observe a proper sequence in the matter of inner healing. For example, the person who has been hurt usually needs to forgive the one who hurt him or her before much inner healing can take place.

Here is a very common sequence:

☐ get in touch with the pain
☐ identify the behavioral cause of the pain
☐ express the pain freely
☐ forgive the one who hurt you
☐ ask Jesus to manifest his presence in the hurtful event and heal you

In our experience, a person may go for months without any conscious prayer for inner healing and then need weekly prayer sessions for a time. In other words, inner healing seems to run on its own calendar. It is a process, but rarely a single event.

Inner healing is the healing of memories. An event can only hurt you once. It is the memory of the event that continues to hurt you. In fact, memory is so powerful that it must be addressed with the grace of God or its negative effects will continue. Though the passage of time helps dull the pain of a memory, time does not of itself dissolve it. We have prayed for people with sixty-year-old emotional wounds that were still having a powerful negative impact.

Inner healing is the application of forgiveness. Too often our spiritual disciplines are dispensed too quickly, before they have the opportunity to touch us at the core of our beings. Many, many persons have been healed of self-inflicted damage to their self-image by simply taking the time to let Jesus come to them . . . hold them . . . express his forgiveness to them . . . and assure them of his limitless love. That probably can't happen in just two minutes. The process is simply one of confession and forgiveness, but it has the *effect* of an inner healing if we take enough time to really internalize what Jesus is doing for us. In a church service, a sixty-second confessional prayer followed by a thirty-second statement of absolution may not provide enough time for the Spirit to massage the loving grace of God into a guilty and wounded heart.

Inner healing is a means of grace through which God demonstrates his sovereignty over the past, inaccessible as it seems. In the mercy of

God, spilled milk can be taken care of. God is Lord over time, not in submission to it. And he is faithful to manifest his presence in accord with his promise "Surely I am with you always, to the very end of the age" (Mt 28:20). We can learn to allow his presence and grace to address the results of specific traumatic events in the past so that they no longer have the capacity to hurt and enslave us in the present.

Finally, inner healing is a set of dynamics and procedures by which to invite the Lord Jesus to address the emotional damage in our lives. The dynamics are based on Scripture; the procedures have been learned from the Spirit in face-to-face ministry situations.

Those who seek to minister inner healing need to know and respect the dynamics. They will be explained in various parts of this book. The procedures have been discovered, pioneered, modified and handed down since the late 1950s, though as we shall see they follow in a centuries-long Christian tradition of spiritual direction. The Spirit is refining and adding to them all the time, as he has done with all other ministries.

In summary, let's propose this definition: inner healing is a method of prayer by which Jesus Christ is invited to address the hurts of the past and heal us of their negative results.

What Inner Healing Is Not

Now let's clarify further by explaining what inner healing is *not.* First, it is not *psychiatry.* The insights and dynamics of psychiatry are far more complex than those needed for effective inner healing. Whereas psychiatry seeks to analyze the past causal factors in a person's personality and behavior, inner healing seeks merely to request the healing touch of Jesus on the past, leaving its analysis to him. Psychiatry seeks the why; inner healing touches the what. Psychiatry, it should be said, can be an exceptionally helpful component in the inner healing of difficult cases.

Further, inner healing is not *positive thinking.* While inner healing may make use of confident expressions of faith, it is not essentially a positive mindset. Positive thinking is a powerful tool; we know that it affects brain chemistry, which produces positive emotions, which further affect brain chemistry. This positive cycle has its counterpart in the negative: negative thoughts produce altered brain chemicals, which depress emotions, which in turn encourage more negative thoughts. But inner healing, while wonderfully positive, is not invested in methods of positive thinking.

Inner healing is not a new way to *meditate.* The person seeking healing certainly benefits from pondering God's healing love for us, but that is only one part of the process. I have experienced inner healings from meditating on Scripture, but it was the active presence of Jesus that accomplished the healing, not the act of meditating.

Nor is inner healing *escapism.* There is the solid expectation that the ministry of inner healing will bring relief to people's inner hurts, but inner healing's method is to penetrate those hurts with the help of Jesus rather than avoid, deny or escape them.

Inner healing is not *group therapy.* While it is incarnational—that is, it is ministered through people—inner healing is not a group enterprise. Even when done in a crowd, it centers on an encounter of the individual with the risen Jesus. What's more, it does not offer the same treatment of problems, the same solutions or the same kind of caring as group therapy. Inner healing requires the power of Jesus to enter the heart and work a change.

Inner healing is not *grief work,* though it candidly addresses the causes of grief in a person's life. Again, in true inner healing the presence and power of Jesus are essential, whereas legitimate grief work can proceed with an appropriate combination of insights and expression of emotion along the stages of adaptation to the loss of a loved one.

Inner healing is not a *recovery program,* though it appreciates and shares some of the assumptions that Twelve-Step programs use. The dynamics of recovery programs are being documented more and more, and one can see the hand of God in their development and use. But inner healing is generally quicker, more individually oriented, more Jesus-centered and more dependent on the power of God.

Inner healing is not *salvation,* though the saving grace of God is never very far from those who are in the healing process and we have known of several persons who came to salvation through the ministry of inner healing. Inner healing is a particularized application of God's grace to a person's emotional life, but this application does not automatically follow after the person has confessed Jesus Christ as Savior and Lord.

Inner healing is not *New Age.* The New Age, holistic spirituality and human potential movements are forms of false religion which focus on untapped resources within the self and hold out the deceptive promise of wholeness. In reality they draw on occult sources of power, offering a counterfeit satisfaction of spiritual hunger and leaving people worse off than before. It is essential to submit inner healing, or any other kind of prayer, to the Scriptures, the guidance of the Holy Spirit, the authority of Jesus and the protection of the Father.

Finally, inner healing is not a *panacea.* While it can release us from the grip of damaged emotions, reduce the impetus to sin, refocus our relationships and refresh our faith, it is not a replacement for the disciplines of sanctification. It does not do away with the need for worship, study, fellowship, good works and prayer.

Once I overheard a young man exclaim that inner healing was "the greatest thing since sliced bread." Not so. *Jesus* is the greatest thing before and since sliced bread!

A Spreading Movement

What we are calling inner healing has, of course, been practiced in the church for centuries under the rubric of "spiritual direction." In recent times the ministry of inner healing has grown out of a number of different traditions which have been influenced by the Pentecostal movement. In the late 1960s the Pentecostal experience leavened many of the mainline churches in what is called the charismatic renewal. Interestingly, the more liturgical arms of the church seemed to pioneer the methods of inner healing that are most in use today. Roman Catholics such as Michael Scanlan, Francis MacNutt and Barbara Schlemon,

Episcopalians such as Leanne Payne and Rita Bennett, Methodist names such as Tommy Tyson and David Seamands, and UCC members such as John and Paula Sandford have all been important in this ministry.

With the move of the Holy Spirit in more evangelical churches, inner healing has made its way there too. At present there is an enormous amount of cross-pollination occurring through books, intensive training seminars, and local and regional grassroots connections. One can find the ministry of inner healing in nearly every type of believing Christian denomination, whether it has a charismatic, evangelical or liturgical approach.

But though this ministry has become widespread, it is still not nearly as extensive as the need demands. What's more, as is common in the development of any spontaneous movement, there are wide variations of biblical, theological, social and psychological expertise, experience and standards.

Signs of a Need for Inner Healing

It would be easy to construct a list of every conceivable malady of the human heart and present it as an indicator of needs for inner healing. This section will conclude with a fairly thorough list. But it can be simpler than that. Early on in this ministry, I noticed that four factors came up again and again and that they produced four results. The four factors are past hurts, fears, guilts and lacks, in various combinations. The four results are negative effects on present self-image, feelings, attitudes and behaviors.

A past rejection—a hurt—can exercise a damaging effect on the person's self-image until it is met with the healing and accepting love of Jesus. You may think of yourself as a person who deserves only rejection because you were rejected by a significant person in the past. The hurt and fear of a woman who has been raped may have led to negative attitudes toward men in general. A fear of heights embedded itself in my emotions because my father held me over a cliff at Yosemite. Many rough-and-tumble street fighters are expressing their childhood hurts and lacks through their belligerence.

A frequent indicator of a need for inner healing is depression, which many psychologists say is *the* major debilitating condition among North Americans. Because any combination of causes can result in depression, it can be challenging to unravel the origins and interrelationships of those causes in order to address them with the power of Jesus. We know, for example, that past hurts can magnify themselves in a person's current thinking, crowding out balancing factors and crystallizing into exclusively negative conclusions about oneself; these thoughts trigger changes in brain chemistry, which further support negative thinking, which brings depression, which flips into a new cycle of the same effects, each of which deepens the depression.

Sometimes physical illnesses are indicators of a need for inner healing, especially when they do not respond to normally effective treatments. A damaged subconscious may not *allow* the body to get well until the emotional damage is healed. When you realize that the subconscious controls all of the involuntary functions of the body—including heartbeat, respiration, hormone secretion, digestion and neural activity—it becomes obvious why it is very important to seek Jesus' healing power for wounded emotions.

What do I mean by the fourth factor in my list, "lacks"? Lacks are good things that should have happened but didn't. Those who practice counseling are finding that one of the chief causes of addictive behavior, besides the already recognized factor of emotional damage, is emotional starvation. This produces a deep hunger for the thing that one has been denied, especially as a child. The driving need for satisfying these hungers may propel the emotionally starved person into addictive behaviors.

In response to the alcoholic we may say, "Just stop drinking!" But our focus on the addictive behavior misses the underlying issue of its cause. When men and women who are compulsive about masturbation or illicit sex get in touch with their past lacks, they often realize that what drives their behavior is the emotional need to be comforted.

Is illicit sexual behavior sin? Yes, and this adds to their discomfort. Do they need forgiveness? Yes. But they also need some way to address the starvation that prompted the self-comforting illicit behavior. When a process of inner healing addresses the emotional lacks in one's past, the impetus to certain addictive sins is dramatically reduced; and this becomes the "way out" of temptation that the Lord promised us (1 Cor 10:13).

In table 1 we elaborate on the causal factors indicating need for inner healing, along with the frequent results of each. We list the results that are most common, but do remember that any result can come from almost any factor or combination of factors.

Table 1. Factors Indicating the Need for Inner Healing

Factors	Results
HURT	Rejection, abandonment, unwantedness; physical, sexual or emotional abuse
FEAR	Anxiety, terror; fear of abandonment, rejection, intimacy; unreasonable fear of almost anything
GUILT	Shame, humiliation, inadequacy, inferiority, sense of unworthiness; self-rejection, negative self-image, disappointment, regret, confusion
ANGER	Hatred, rage, bitterness, resentment; unforgiveness, stubbornness, rebellion, critical spirit; anger at God, others, self; depression, suicide
LUST	Sexual immorality, pornography, substance abuse; jealousy, possessiveness
LACK (of love, acceptance, intimacy, affirmation)	Any of the results above, culminating in an inability to love and trust God and others

Looking Ahead

And now we shall begin exploring these possibilities and problems in greater depth. We will tell you how we became involved in this ministry. Then we will delve into the theological and scriptural underpinnings of inner healing. Following that we will take two chapters to lay out six key principles or dynamics of inner healing.

With this groundwork in place, you will be ready to deal with the specific processes of praying for yourself and others and to understand psychological factors, frequent mistakes, how to collaborate more effectively with the Holy Spirit and how to deal with the presence of evil. Along the way we hope to respond straightforwardly to concerns and questions that many Christians have about inner healing.

2

HOW WE BECAME INVOLVED IN INNER HEALING

We'd like to take a few pages to tell you how the Lord got us both involved in inner healing, because we suspect that you'll be able to identify with one or the other of us. Two more different entrances to the same ministry could hardly be imagined. The common factor between us is that neither of us sought it.

Doug's Story
"Holy Spirit, what are the roots of these fears and doubts that are troubling Doug?"

It was early February 1987. My friend Gordon was praying for me at the close of a counseling session; I had been speaking with him about unreasonable fears and doubts I was having at work. As Gordon invited the Spirit's presence, I suddenly remembered an early teenage experience.

During a family dinner, my father, in reaction to my older sister's rebellious taunts, had thrown a glass of milk against the fireplace and shouted with uncontrollable anger and rage at her. Then, in shame and despair, he had locked himself in his study. His sobs and groans echoed through the house. As I remembered that event, I felt again the terror of seeing my father out of control.

"What's happening, Doug?" Gordon asked me as we remained in an attitude of prayer. I shared the memory. Then we took time to ask Jesus to be there—in the memory—and to show me where he was and what he was doing during that painful episode.

A wonderful thing happened as I opened my heart to the Lord in faith: *Jesus was there!* It's hard to describe the impact of that simple awareness. He came alongside me to calm the fear and confusion and to help me see the memory in a different light. He showed me his compassionate heart of love for my father, who was sick and troubled in his own emotions and spirit.

"I sense that the Lord wants you to speak to your father," Gordon nudged. "Is there anything that you want to say to him?"

I had never consciously thought of this, but as my friend asked the question, my insides exploded.

"Dad! Why did you do it? *Why did you kill yourself?*"

I was suddenly, emotionally, right back at that very moment in the summer of 1960—twenty-seven years before, when I was eighteen—when my uncle's voice came over the phone: "Doug, your father is dead. He died yesterday. He took his own life."

"No! No!" I shouted in anger. I desperately wanted to deny it.

After I hung up the phone, I couldn't help repeating over and over, "Why, Dad? Why did you do it?" I cried for a while. Then, in a moment of calculated finality, I pushed all the feelings and questions down, down, down. I couldn't, or wouldn't, cry or express emotion again, even at the funeral.

I survived the summer and returned to college for my sophomore year, picking up the pieces of my life as best I could. But I felt cheated, robbed: I had been just on the verge of coming into an adult relationship with my father, and now he was gone.

Following college I married Judy, went to seminary and became associate pastor of a suburban church in Southern California. I stayed in that position for five years before returning to graduate school for a doctorate in social ethics. In 1974, at age thirty-three, I became chaplain and professor of religious studies at a small liberal arts college in Los Angeles. Through the influence of faithful students, I came into a deeper, personal, loving relationship with Jesus. And I began to experience the power and guidance of the Holy Spirit.

Within a few years the Spirit began to nudge me about my father's death. I would think about him at odd moments and feel twinges of regret at losing him. I visited his grave several times, experiencing a sense of both peace and expectancy.

During those years I began to come to grips with my fears and anxieties. My fears were out of proportion to what was actually happening in my life: I was overly fearful of displeasing people, of not being liked or approved. And I was unreasonably afraid that I would commit suicide at age fifty, just as my father had.

In the mid 1980s I began to see more clearly the need for healing of emotional hurts from the past. I learned that many of our seemingly most difficult problems, compulsions, fears and emotional difficulties are results of deep long-term wounds. I realized more fully that we are deeply affected by things that have happened to us, by the sins of others and by evil in the world.

I had grown up in a happy home. I had two loving parents and all the blessings and opportunities anyone could ask for. I did not experience the traumas of divorce, murder, sexual abuse, abandonment or rejection. And yet this fairly "normal" childhood had produced wounds from seemingly simple things: a sense of failure from not making the Little League team, a fear of surgery on my front teeth, inadequacy at not being able to gain weight after the eighth grade, jealousy of a friend's success, hatred and anger resulting from a betrayal, shame from hidden sin, and after age eighteen, fear and depression resulting from my father's death.

The Holy Spirit began to bring these memories and the emotions attached to them to the surface through intercessory prayer and inner healing. But it all came to a head with Gordon in that prayer session in 1987.

"Why, Dad? Why did you do it?" I burst out with years of repressed anger and pain.

Then the presence of Jesus began to heal me. He gave me his compassion for my father. I saw how sick and helpless Dad had been, how hard he had tried and how very, very tired he had been. I found myself saying, "Dad, I love you, I forgive you. I miss you, Dad!"

I was giving expression to all the things I had wanted to say to my father twenty-seven years before, things I had wanted to say to him while he was still alive, things I had needed to say to him after his death. Healing was taking place in my wounded heart.

I had thought that was all I needed. But a few months later, at a healing conference led by Francis and Judith MacNutt, I had a vision of my father. He was standing before me, about fifteen feet away. Eager to be with him, I dashed toward him, but as I ran he receded into the distance.

I cried out, "Jesus, help me!" Then Jesus appeared from the left, went to my father and brought him to me. The three of us hugged. Nothing was said, but I had a deep sense that my father knew Jesus and that I could trust Jesus to be in charge. I sensed that I would see my father in heaven and that it would be a glorious reunion. And the love of my heavenly Father continued to heal me of the loss of my earthly father's love.

Surely, I thought, *I'm totally healed now.* But in the fall of that year, as I was talking to my oldest son, John—who was beginning his sophomore year in college—I was flooded by the realization that I was now experiencing with my son the very things that my father had missed with me. I was filled with an awareness of my father's love for me, the same love I was now feeling for my own son. I choked up and began to cry quietly.

God used that event to overcome more of the hurt I had experienced from my father's death. In particular, he filled in the lack of my father's presence over the years.

I thought this must be the completion of the healing. But at Christmas dinner that year, my mom brought out an old Christmas sermon Dad had written, and she proposed that we read it aloud. I could not read my part. Instead I excused myself, went to my room and cried for twenty minutes—talking to Jesus, talking to my father, emptying out a depth of emotion that surprised me. This release brought a deepened inner freedom from fear and anxiety and a growing confidence and trust in our loving God.

From my experience of healing I learned that we may need to be touched at successive levels by the healing power of Jesus. It is possible that there are yet undiscovered dimensions of the pain of my father's death that I have to be healed of. But I know from my own experience that our God is eager and able to heal the most difficult of past events.

It is my testimony that God's very nature is to overcome darkness with light and pain with healing. I believe that he is already at work to bring each of us to strength and wholeness, and that inner healing is one of the means by which "in all things God works for the good of those who love him, who have been called according to his purpose" (Rom 8:28). I know from my own experience that *nothing* "will be able to separate us from the love of God that is in Christ Jesus our Lord" (Rom 8:39).

In the years since 1987 I have gained experience and knowledge in the ministry of inner healing. Over a two-year stretch the Holy Spirit took me in hand and Jesus became my teacher, giving me experience after experience of praying for people with the blessing of his direct and immediate guidance. As the Lord released me into this ministry, he spoke to me quite clearly from Scripture, "You did not choose me, but I chose you and appointed you to go and bear fruit—fruit that will last. Then the Father will give you whatever you ask in my name. This is my command: Love each other" (Jn 15:16-17).

God wants us to know how much he loves us. If we can't get an awareness of his love through our parents, we can receive it from him through inner healing. He is the only one who can meet the deepest needs of our hearts.

Once we receive his love and know our worth in him, we have freedom from inner bondage. That is the heart of inner healing: letting Jesus come close enough to take away the pain and hurt, learning to trust him enough to put everything in his hands.

The good news is that our great God is at work to heal us, to bring us salvation, to bring us into wholeness. When Jesus took our infirmities upon himself on the cross, he gained the right to heal us. He will take pain and fear and rejection and replace them with his healing and peace and acceptance, bringing us into the inner freedom of abundant life.

Mike's Story

"I want to pray for you, young man. You just sit here in this chair. I'll stand behind you and place my hands on your head and pray. I want to alert you that I shake when I pray, so don't be alarmed by that manifestation."

Wondering what I had gotten myself into, I sat down as instructed, and she placed her hands on the top of my head. Sure enough, after a few seconds her hands began to shake. Quite forcefully.

At first I couldn't figure out how to cooperate with her. I didn't know whether to stiffen my neck and resist the shaking or relax and go along with it. I'd never even seen anyone shake like that, much less experienced the shaking so personally, for her shaking became mine as my head bobbed about.

Meanwhile a torrent of words was pouring forth from her lips. As I became aware of the intent of those words, I became upset. Had I not felt constrained by the need to be polite, I would have held up my hand in a "stop-this" posture, for I heard her say, "And Lord, I ask you to give Mike my anointing for healing of memories."

Two things about that sentence bothered me. I had never heard the word *anointing* used in this way. What could she possibly mean by such a request? What was an anointing? What was *her* anointing? And how could she give it to me? Worse, she was asking that this mysterious anointing should in some way relate to the business of "healing of memories," and I had already decided I wanted nothing whatever to do with that.

I should clarify that a mere twenty-one months before—in August 1972—I had experienced a complete reorientation of my life and ministry through an unsought spiritual renewal. At the age of thirty-one, I had been a rather ineffective pastor in the Episcopal Church in California for six years. That I needed renewing was beyond question. I gladly accepted this blessing. But it was the accouterments of renewal that I was twitchy about. Did I *have* to speak in tongues or heal the sick or look silly in worship? Why couldn't I just do the more normal-looking things like teach, preach, lead and help? For after my renewal I had begun learning about these things.

I put some of the practices I heard about on my "not ever" list. At the top of that list was the phrase *healing of memories.*

I had heard the phrase from the people I'd begun associating with, and had taken an instant dislike to it. The Lord had turned so much of my life upside down that I just didn't need any more new and weird things. If it was valid for someone's memories to be healed—whatever that could possibly mean—let someone else do it, not me. Consequently I had learned nothing about this sort of healing. But now this famous woman, Agnes Sanford, was praying in the study of her hillside home that I would be given her anointing for the thing that seemed the weirdest of all weird "Holy Spirit" phenomena.

Fortunately, the prayer ended after a couple of minutes. As quickly as I could, I excused myself and made for the front door, eager to get out of there. But one last weirdness awaited me before I made my exit: Agnes Sanford's companion, Edith Drury, appeared by the front door. As we met, she sized me up and somewhat gruffly observed to Agnes that I "just might make it." Something in the way she said it made me feel like a kindergartner who might be encouraged to try to erase the blackboard by himself.

As my car pulled away from the curb, I exhaled long and forcefully, thinking, "Well, that session was a dead loss!" And I pondered what could have possessed me to have made the appointment in the first place. It was only seven miles from Sanford's house in Monrovia to my church in El Monte, but by the time I got back I had completely dismissed the encounter as a fluke.

Exactly one week later, a woman sat in my office and tried to articulate why she couldn't get over a painful episode with her husband which had occurred six years earlier. It appeared that his rejection of her was an isolated event, that it had never happened before or since. But she couldn't get it out of her mind, and it kept her from fully trusting her husband, much as she wanted to.

"Why can't I just get over it?" she lamented.

Since my renewal, I had been in the habit of practicing the presence of Jesus by envisioning him on a throne wherever I went, every time I thought of it. I wanted him to be the Lord, sovereign over any situation in which I found myself, and over my actions. Now, through sheer force of habit, I glanced up toward him, for I didn't know how to respond to this woman's dilemma.

"She needs healing of memories," he said in my mind.

Oh Lord, I groaned silently, *I told you I don't want to do that!*

"But she needs it."

But I don't want to do it.

"But she needs it."

But Lord—

"Who *is* Lord, Mike?"

He had me there. So I sighed resignedly and said to the woman, "I think what you need is healing of memories."

"That's fine with me," she replied. "What *is* healing of memories?"

Suddenly I was faced with the embarrassment of not knowing one single thing about a ministry I had just told someone she needed. Using the old ruse of the person who wants to convey urgency, I glanced at my watch; then I said, "Well, never mind about the explanation. Let's just pray."

As she bowed her head, I fastened my attention again on Jesus, crying silently, "Help!"

And then, in the soft, flicky way the imagination works, I saw Jesus get down off his throne and kneel on one knee to the woman's left. He placed his right arm around her shoulders in a comforting manner. Then he took his left hand and reached into her heart, extracting a large lump of what looked like black Jell-O. He placed the gelatinous mass in his own heart, where it immediately began to shrink until it vanished. Then he reached into his heart, extracting a lump of milk-white gelatin, the same size and shape as the black had been. This he carefully inserted into the woman's heart.

Having finished this transaction, he turned to face me and said, "Do that."

Oh great! I lamented to myself. *How am I going to do that?* But having nothing else to go on, I opened my mouth and began to pray.

Over the next few moments, several minor miracles occurred. First, I realized that I had to pray about the episode in which the woman's husband had rejected her. Before I could protest in my mind that the event was in the past and therefore closed, a clear thought on the Hebrew concept of contemporaneity of times came to mind. I hadn't thought of such things since seminary days. But the Lord used that concept to show me that he is Lord over time and could, as a matter of fact, "go into" the past with his grace. I knew, however, that I could not ask him to change this woman's history, but rather to heal it.

So I prayed, "Lord Jesus, I ask you to go back in the past to the time when this lady's husband hurt her. I don't ask you to keep it from happening, Lord; I just ask you to heal her of it. So after he said those things and pushed her to the floor, I ask you to enter the room and approach her. I ask you, Jesus, to lift her to her feet and put your arms around her. Please comfort her, Jesus. After a while, I ask you to reach into her heart and take away a large lump of black Jell-O." Here I sneaked a look to see if she was rolling her eyes in derision, but she was obviously engaged in prayer. "Whew!" I thought, "we're home free!"

I continued praying: "Lord, put this black Jell-O, which represents the hurt and rejection she experienced, into your own heart." At that instant, this sentence from Matthew 8:17 came to mind: "He took our infirmities and bore our diseases" (RSV). With a shock, I realized that Jesus was saying to this woman that he had personally experienced her pain when he was on the cross.

As I said that aloud, I heard her begin to weep softly. "Lord," I went on, "when you died, this pain died. And when you rose from the dead, you rose free and clear of it, having left it in hell where it originated and where it belongs. Now, Lord, I ask you to represent your victory over this hurt by reaching into your heart again and taking out milk-white Jell-O, the same size and shape as the black had been. Place this, which represents your healing, into her heart. Whereas the black Jell-O was rejection, let this white Jell-O be acceptance. Let hurt be replaced with healing. Let darkness be replaced with light."

And then I surprised myself one last time: "Lord, I declare that the memory of this event will never again hurt this lady or damage her relationship with her husband. Amen!"

Where did I get off saying that? I wondered to myself, but the woman's behavior took my attention from that question. She was saying things like "Oh thank you, Jesus. Oh, I'm healed! I'm OK now. Oh thank you, Lord!"

I didn't want to look like a doubting Thomas, so I kept quiet as she picked up her purse, thanked me profusely and left. But I was thinking, *How did she* know *that she was healed? Was she really healed, or was she trying to make me feel better for having tried? She certainly gave the impression of having been healed. What happened here? And if something real happened,* how *did it happen?*

But as the event receded in time, so did my questions. In fact, I was glad to have escaped from the unnerving encounter without botching things up. I fervently expected that this was a fluke—a once-in-a-lifetime kind of fluke—which I, thankfully, would never have to repeat. That was the first week of June 1974.

I have rarely been more mistaken in my understanding of the Lord's plans for me. Within weeks I was praying for more and more people. By August I was well along in the matter of learning what we now call inner healing, praying for several people a week.

Each person I prayed with taught me something about this ministry. All I had to do was listen to them, look at Jesus and pray as he seemed to lead. Finally, after praying for scores of people, I decided to do some reading to see if I was on target with what other people thought about this ministry. As I read, another miracle slowly dawned on me: the books and articles showed me that the Lord had taught me almost all the basics of this ministry without input from anyone else, for little that I read was new or unexperienced. And the methods I had been led to use were confirmed.

Meanwhile, I began to seek my own inner healing. I had had the good fortune to be raised in a fairly healthy family. My family certainly wasn't flawless, but I had few traumas that needed the healing touch of Jesus. At that time I didn't know many people who were ministering inner healing, so I began to pray for myself. The style of doing it was something I just fell into: I prayed for myself in the same way I prayed for others. I would take the position of an observer, as it were, seeing Jesus approach the little boy I had been and heal him of some hurt. This third-person manner of prayer seemed to work as well for myself as for others.

Once when the Lord had told me to put my job on the line because of a point of disagreement,[1] he healed me of the fear of financial need which had hindered my obedience to his directions. After praying for the healing of that fear, I found that it was possible to confront the disagreement, even if it meant losing my job.

After three years, I had prayed for several hundred persons and was spending up to twenty hours a week doing inner healing. I began to realize that this could not continue as a one-man show. I did, after all, have a parish to run.

Renewal groups had asked me to speak on inner healing in 1975 and 1976. Preparing for those talks did much to clarify and organize my thinking about the dynamics and methods of inner healing. I also became aware that others could be trained to exercise this ministry. And surprise of surprises, I even ended up laying hands on them and praying that the Lord would anoint them with the power to heal. What a sense of humor the Lord has! At least he didn't make me shake.

* * *

Our two stories show that the Lord gets some people into inner healing through their need to receive it and some through their need to give it. Either way, we have found it a rich blessing in our lives and ministries. And in the next two chapters Doug will lay out the theological and scriptural foundations for this ministry.

3

THEOLOGICAL UNDERPINNINGS

For *the past twenty years I (Doug) have been in ministry to college* students as a chaplain, professor, pastor and counselor. Over this time I have been particularly impressed by young people's deep need to know and experience the love of God in concrete, tangible ways. Many students who come to me for counseling and prayer are in bondage from childhood experiences of physical, sexual and emotional abuse, abandonment, self-hatred, depression and temptations to suicide. And I have seen them wonderfully freed by the loving, healing presence of Jesus. The terrible things that happen to children in our broken world *can be overcome and healed* through the love and power of Jesus.

My closest interactions with children have been with my own three children. My wife, Judy, and I adopted our middle child, Sarah, when she was only a few weeks old. From the earliest days we talked in positive terms with her about how we "chose her" and how pleased we were to have her in our family. But the day came when it dawned on her that her natural birth mother "gave me away."

Increasingly Sarah felt that she had been abandoned and unwanted. She would constantly ask about her natural mother (though we had little information to give her) and fantasize what life with her "real mom" would be like. Over a three- to four-year period it seemed to us that an evil presence was growing in Sarah. She tested us, sometimes beyond our patience and understanding. We tried to show her and tell her that she was loved, that she was valuable and loved by God and by us, but there seemed to be a war going on within her, and we often felt powerless to break through with God's love and truth.

This all came to a head one day following an argument between Sarah and Judy. In anger, they went off in different directions down the upstairs hallway. Sarah went into her bedroom and slammed the door. Judy pounded her fist against the linen-closet door and cried out, "Oh God, help me!"

At that, Sarah popped her head out of her door and snarled, "If I'm so bad, why don't you just give me back?"

Judy whipped around and responded firmly, "I am not that other mother! We don't give our pets away, we don't give our children away. We can learn to get along or we can hate each other, but you are stuck with us for life!"

Something broke in Sarah, and she ran to Judy, threw herself in her mother's arms and cried out, "I love you, Mommy!"

From that day Sarah's actions and attitudes were different. The presence of evil we had sensed in her was gone. Emotional healing had occurred, grounded in the love of God and ministered through a loving mother. A crucial battle had been won, and the victory was stronger self-identity and self-acceptance for Sarah.

But what actually happened? Was this a genuine act of God? Or was it simply the result of a persistent mom and luck? Was this inner healing? How do we know? How is inner healing rooted in our understanding of God and his purposes for humankind?

In this chapter we will identify the theological underpinnings and structures that can give us confidence in talking about God's ministry of inner healing from emotional damage, childhood trauma and the consequences of human sin. Theology, simply understood, is our human attempt to understand the character, mind and purposes of God and the way he plans for us to live in fellowship with himself and one another. Let's begin.

The Character of God

God desires that his name be known in all the earth (Ps 46:10), that his name be a praise in all the earth (Ps 148; 150; Rom 14:11) and that we rejoice in him and glory in his name (Is 41:16; 48:9-11; Zech 10:12). But what is his name? God proclaimed to Moses that he was the great "I AM," the living God (Ex 3:14), "the compassionate and gracious God, slow to anger, abounding in love and faithfulness, maintaining love to thousands, and forgiving wickedness, rebellion and sin" (Ex 34:6-7).

The Bible characteristically uses intimate terms to speak about God. He is the loving Father. Even more warm and intimate, he is our Husband. In a marriage ceremony, the bride and groom call each other by name: "I, Doug, take you, Judy, to be my lawful wedded wife . . ." Husband-God says the same words of promise and endearment to his people: "I have called you by name. . . . You are precious in my sight, and honored, and I love you" (Is 43:1-4 NRSV). At times he uses another metaphor with warm overtones to describe his relationship with us: "He tends his flock like a shepherd: He gathers the lambs in his arms and carries them close to his heart; he gently leads those that have young" (Is 40:11).

In other words, God generously identifies himself with the welfare of his people, and here he discloses his heart of genuine love. Can you see yourself as his child, his bride, his lamb?

God's purpose for his people is right relationship with himself and with each other—thus the two great commands to "love the Lord your God . . . [and] your neighbor as yourself" (Mk 12:30-31; see also Lev

19:18; Deut 6:5). Complete well-being is God's intent for man and woman in all aspects of our lives—spiritual, physical and emotional. The Hebrew word *shalom* is best understood as meaning "soundness" or "well-being," with connection between physical and emotional health and ethical and spiritual obedience (see Ex 15:26; Deut 28:58-61).[1]

However, sin separates us from God and keeps us from his promised shalom. Righteousness and holiness are also central to God's character. Though he promises to forgive wickedness, rebellion and sin, "he does not leave the guilty unpunished; he punishes the children and their children for the sin of the fathers to the third and fourth generation" (Ex 34:7). To come more fully into God's shalom, we must allow him to deal with our sin and brokenness and to remold us into a holy and righteous people.

Our Problem

God's love and compassion, his good purposes for creation and human-kind, were challenged by the human decision to rebel and refuse God's good provision. Our first parents set themselves up against God, ex-pressing distrust in him by seeking to secure their own futures in con-tradiction to his explicit commands and warnings. The earliest chapters in the Bible provide a portrait of the fall of human beings from God's will and intent to a state of sin and rebellion—the human problem for which the rest of the Bible seeks to provide a solution.

King David laments, "Surely I was sinful at birth, sinful from the time my mother conceived me" (Ps 51:5). He realized that not only had he sinned, but something had gone wrong from the beginning, resulting in a world where humans feel drawn into temptation and sin. "Create in me a pure heart, O God," he cried. "Wash away all my iniquity and cleanse me from my sin" (Ps 51:10, 2).

Jesus, too, knew well what comes from the heart of a person—"evil thoughts, sexual immorality, theft, murder, adultery, greed, malice, de-ceit, lewdness, envy, slander, arrogance and folly" (Mk 7:21-22; see Jer 17:9-10; Mt 23:25; Jn 8:32-36).

The primary consequence of human sin is separation from God. All the other consequences are inevitable byproducts: death, shame, denial, pain, difficult marriage relationships, hard manual labor (Gen 3). Sin abounded as Cain's murder of Abel brought separation and isolation and modeled murder, hatred and vengeance for those who followed (Gen 4:23). The consequences of human sin and rebellion brought judgment from God, for he destroyed most of the human race (Gen 6) and sought to establish a faithful remnant. But rebellion continued in the communal sin of Babel, which brought misunderstanding and enmity among the people groups of the earth (Gen 11). So we see that sin has consequences for the spiritual, physical, emotional and interpersonal dimensions of human life.

Since the Fall, our world is a counterfeit image of the world God made. Adam and Eve, by rebelling against God, delivered themselves and their descendants into the hands of Satan, who exploits human sin and brokenness as a means of securing his position as ruler of this world. Death, shame, denial, disease, emotional sickness, racism—human brokenness in all its dimensions is characteristic of Satan's counterfeit kingdom. Michael Green writes: "Disease and death are all part and parcel of the spurious deal the devil gave in return for primal man's 'yes' to temptation. In some mysterious way sin, disease and death are all part of the heritage of disobedience."[2]

And as Paul writes, "God cannot be mocked. A man reaps what he sows. The one who sows to please his sinful nature, from that nature will reap destruction" (Gal 6:7-8). When we break God's moral laws, we experience sure and certain consequences. We reap what we sow— every sin bears with it the seeds of destruction for our relationship with God, our relationships with others and our own well-being. Our human tendency is to dismiss or ignore sin, to deny it or refuse to see the connection between sowing and reaping. Often the fruit of sin can come a long time after the sin itself, sometimes not until the Last Judgment.

The prophet Nathan told King David that the consequences of his adultery would include the death of his son, strife with his family and eventually further adulteries and deaths (2 Sam 12:11-14). The death of David's son came immediately. Other family difficulties inevitably followed: the incest of David's son Absalom (2 Sam 13), betrayal and separation between David and Absalom, armed rebellion against David, and eventually Absalom's death in battle (2 Sam 18).

Sin cycles of sowing and reaping come in each of our lives. A young man, Alex, came for counseling during a period of separation from his wife. He was involved with another woman but had dismissed this sin as being of no consequence as he sought his own pleasure. Yet he had become "a different person" and "a dead man" (Eph 2:1-3), according to the testimony of his best friends. As we talked, he told me that he felt hopeless about change because he had always felt the powerful temptation of lust and the lure of sexually explicit photos and films. With this confession it became clear that Alex was now reaping the consequences of others' sins and sowing new sins to continue the sin cycle in his own life and the lives of others.

We reap from the sins of others as well as our own. As I pointed out already, our righteous and holy God "punishes the children and their children for the sin of the fathers to the third and fourth generation" (Ex 34:7). Absalom was affected by David's sin. Alex was affected by sins of adultery and promiscuity in his family line. My daughter Sarah was affected by the sins and choices of her natural parents. This may seem unfair, as though we have been set up to fail; but God has created us to receive what comes from the hands and lives of our parents and relatives. As our first parents fell into sin and rebellion, they opened the way for us to receive evil along with good, leaving us to struggle and deal in our own lives with the consequences of sin.

And struggle we do! We often freely choose to continue in the sin patterns that are pressing on us; and we reject and rebel against the best efforts and intentions of parents and family.[3] It is our rebellion and our reaction to sin that causes permanent damage in our lives. The spiritual impact of others' sin on our lives is our responsibility. Even if we have been the victim of the worst possible circumstances, we are still responsible in some measure for *our response*—whether we choose to move into an unreal world, to hate or resent, or to forgive and let go of bitter judgments.[4]

Sin brings consequences that affect our thinking, feeling and acting. If we feed our minds with lies and distortions, as King David did regarding Uriah's wife, Bathsheba, our emotions become sick and our wills weak. If we believe and act as though God were not trustworthy, as did Adam and Eve, then our thinking and attitudes about ourselves and others become sick, and we fall prey to further lies of the enemy. If we focus on moral filth and pornographic images, as Alex did, our conscience or moral sense is dulled, and we cannot distinguish between good and evil, love and lust; we become emotional cripples. If we experience rejection or abandonment in childhood, as Sarah did, this sets up a wrong view of ourselves, the world and God. The distortion and destruction that come from our own sin and the sin of others needs to be understood and dealt with if we are to grow into the health God desires for us.

What a frightening picture of the destructiveness of sin! We are overwhelmed by sin cycles in our families, childhood trauma and abuse, our responses to those hurts, the lure of worldly pleasures, and weakness in our own flesh. Even when we want to do right, evil lies close at hand. Paul knew the war that was going on in his own body, how he felt like "a prisoner of the law of sin at work within my members." No wonder he cried out, "What a wretched man I am! Who will rescue me from this body of death?" (Rom 7:21-24).

God's Solution

Fortunately, Paul's answer was not long in coming: "Thanks be to God— through Jesus Christ our Lord" (Rom 7:25). A rescue is underway from the brokenness at the heart of human history and the human soul. God has done what we, in our weakened and wretched condition, could not do ourselves. He sent his own Son to set us "free from the law of sin and death" (Rom 8:2). Through Jesus' sacrifice we are liberated from the cycles of sin and the inevitability of sin and its consequences. In his death he took upon himself our sins, weaknesses and infirmities (Is 53:4) and won the right to bear the consequences of all the sin we have sown. The most important result of sin—separation from God—is overcome when we put our trust in Jesus (Rom 5:10). Death itself will be remedied at the resurrection.

And what of the other consequences of sin that we Christians continue to experience day by day—bondage from childhood experiences of sexual and emotional abuse, abandonment, self-rejection, anger and hatred, shame, lust and so forth? As we surrender to Jesus, he reaps where we have sown. "By his wounds we are healed" (Is 53:5).

There is tension in the Christian life between the "already and not yet." We are already saved and covered by Jesus' righteousness, "new creations" in Christ (2 Cor 5:17); yet we are still shot through with sin and brokenness, needing to "put to death . . . whatever belongs to [our] earthly nature: sexual immorality, impurity, lust, evil desires and greed . . . anger, rage, malice, slander" (Col 3:5, 8). We live in the midst of God's steadfast love and healing power in the present and await the promise of his full deliverance from our circumstances in the future. So, then, we know that "neither death, nor life, nor angels, nor principalities, nor things present, nor things to come, nor powers, nor height, nor depth, nor anything else in all creation, will be able to separate us from the love of God in Christ Jesus our Lord" (Rom 8:38-39 RSV).

Christ's work is finished and complete, but our sanctification is in process and is therefore partial. Many of our sins and wrong attitudes are cleansed and changed through our initial belief in Christ; others must be taken specifically to the cross in the process of our sanctification. Thus James encourages his flock to "confess your sins to one another, and pray for one another, that you may be healed" (Jas 5:16 RSV).

Emotional healing takes place when we take specific sins, sin patterns and emotional sickness to the cross. Paul helps us see this process of healing and sanctification when he admonishes: "Work out your own salvation with fear and trembling; for God is at work in you, both to will and to work for his good pleasure" (Phil 2:12-13 RSV).

God Desires to Heal Our Sickness

The clearest and fullest view of God's attitude toward our sickness is found in his self-revelation in Jesus Christ. When we look at Jesus, we see the explicit declaration of God's will! Jesus declared that "the Son can do nothing of his own accord, but only what he sees the Father doing; for whatever he does, that the Son does likewise. For the Father loves the Son, and shows him all that he himself is doing" (Jn 5:19-20 RSV). Jesus is absolutely faithful in revealing the Father's will to us— and in his words and actions, he shows the Father's unambiguous hostility toward sin and sickness.

In Jesus we see that God pursues our welfare. God's heart is moved for us, and his power is near to us. Jesus came to preach the gospel of the kingdom, to heal the sick and to cast out demons. His concern is for the whole person. The word that our Bibles translate "salvation" is most often used in the Gospels with reference to the healing of disease. Salvation is the activity of God directed toward those who suffer and are in need of his help.

Upon the Hebrews' deliverance from the tyranny of Pharaoh, God made a promise: "If you listen carefully to the voice of the LORD your God and do what is right in his eyes, if you pay attention to his commands and keep all his decrees, I will not bring on you any of the diseases I brought on the Egyptians, for I am the LORD, who heals you" (Ex 15:26). Healing and salvation are two aspects of God's rescue operation: "Praise the LORD, O my soul . . . who forgives all your sins and heals all your diseases" (Ps 103:2-3). Salvation is spiritual, physical and emotional wholeness—God's shalom.

As Jesus encountered people considered to be unclean in his culture, such as lepers, he healed the physical disease and restored the person to social and cultural relationships. He forgives sins *and* heals the sicknesses associated with them (Mk 2). Jesus is concerned even for our trivial pains and worries—the fever of Peter's mother-in-law, the short-age of wine at a wedding, the multitudes in need of a picnic lunch. He saw the heart and opened the way for the woman caught in adultery (Jn 8), the woman who responded to him by the well in Samaria (Jn 4), Peter trapped in betrayal (Jn 18, 21). On nearly every page of the Gospels we see the deep sympathy of Jesus for people trapped in physical and mental suffering, caught in webs of injustice, with lives marked by sorrow and despair.[5]

Jesus' love and compassion for those trapped in physical and emotional suffering became real for me a few years ago during a trip Mike and I took to Hong Kong. I was praying for a young man who had been abandoned as a child and left to fend for himself in the streets. He became a member of the gangs that controlled prostitution, drug sales and gambling within the walled city of Kowloon. He could not read or write and was paralyzed on his left side from a vicious street fight a few years before. But he was reaching out for the light of Christ.

As I prayed, I asked Jesus to show me how he was at work, how he was praying and interceding for this man. The Spirit gave me a brief but clear impression of Jesus reaching his arms out into ooze and slime to grab and take this man to himself. I saw the aggressive love of Jesus reaching out, intending to snatch and draw this man into himself, to take him into his own body, where his own wounds and stripes would heal the brokenness in body, spirit and emotions. I saw how much God loved this man who could not read or write, who had been involved in the worst kind of sin and degradation, and yet who was made in God's image—and I saw by implication how much God loves each one of us.

The Gospels often tell us that Jesus was "filled with compassion," signifying his deep identification with our pain and suffering. For example: "When Jesus landed and saw a great crowd, he had compassion on them and healed their sick" (Mt 14:14). Like a good shepherd, he is concerned for the welfare of his people (Mk 6:34). Jesus went about preaching and "healing every disease and sickness. When he saw the crowds, he had compassion on them, because they were harassed and helpless, like sheep without a shepherd" (Mt 9:35-36). Jesus' every word and action reflect to us the heart, will and character of God. And what Jesus reveals to us is that the central loving purpose of God is to bring salvation, healing and wholeness to his people.

Our Response
The final part of God's remedy for our sin is our repentance and faith. "The kingdom of God is near," Jesus says. "Repent and believe the good news!" (Mk 1:15). Through the innocent suffering of his own Son on the cross, God's righteous anger at our sin has been satisfied, and we are able, by his redeeming mercy and power, to be reconciled with God. We receive the truth and fruit of Jesus' sacrifice by repenting of our sins, placing our trust and confidence in Jesus and allowing God to change our sinful nature.

In repentance we go to the cross and lay our sins, burdens and weaknesses at the feet of Jesus. There we receive forgiveness from the One who has won our trust by giving his life for us. And we allow our sinful nature to be crucified with him. As Paul says, "I have been crucified with Christ and I no longer live, but Christ lives in me" (Gal 2:20).

Since Christ lives in us, we have the means to deal with ongoing sin and sin patterns. When a sinful habit or act comes to light, we can take it to the cross in prayerful repentance. We admit that we cannot change on our own, and we give control to Jesus. We willingly give our sin over to him and trust him to put it to death. Then we are free to move into more powerful obedience, faithfulness and righteousness by the power of the indwelling Spirit.

Jesus came also to ignite faith, trust and confidence in his loving Father. "Your faith has healed you," he said, and "Have faith!" (Mk 5:34; 11:22). Today it is still our response of faith in him that enables his saving, healing love and power to flow to us and through us.

Healing comes as a corollary of relationship with God. The key question for us, then, is whether God is the sort of being we can trust and with whom we can be vulnerable. And the answer is an emphatic *yes* in Jesus Christ. "All the promises of God find their Yes in him" (2 Cor 1:20 RSV).

In Jesus we have a safe place to come and wrestle through our fears and angers, shames and hurts.

"God, why did you let my father die?"

"Why did you allow my uncle to molest me?"

"Why did you give me these indifferent parents?"

So much of our anger and hurt is finally directed at God. If my heavenly father is sovereign and knows everything about me and everything that is happening, where was he when I was in so much pain and torment? What was he doing? And why didn't he prevent those things from happening? As we dare to bring these questions to him in prayer for emotional healing, we discover that he has protected us in ways we did not understand and won the right on the cross to cleanse, heal, restore and redeem us from even the worst of circumstances. It becomes an experiential fact that "in everything God works for good with those who love him, who are called according to his purpose" (Rom 8:28 RSV).

In a recent inner healing prayer session, my friend Joanne struggled with God about the anger and fear she felt because of hurts inflicted by the parents he had given her. Could she trust God to care for her? As we prayed and asked Jesus to be present, we both had very clear impressions that he was indeed present and that a wrestling match was unfolding. Suddenly I saw Joanne pin Jesus to the floor. She had his wrists caught, and as she looked down into his loving face, he laughed and said, "You've got me. Now what are you going to do?"

The scene was so incongruous that both Joanne and I began to laugh. But Jesus said to her: "Joanne, I've been vulnerable to you on the cross. I gave my life for you so that you could belong completely to me. You can trust me, because I love you enough to have died for you! Now, can you be vulnerable to me? Can you trust me and let *me* pin *you?*"

And then Jesus waited for Joanne to respond in faith and trust. As she said yes to Jesus—and repented of the fears and anger against God—Jesus picked her up, held her, hugged her and spoke to her about her parents and about events from the past. Joanne was able to experience some of Jesus' heart of compassion toward her parents and to begin the process of forgiveness and healing.

Our experience in praying for others has shown us that people who have trouble trusting God, who are unable to be vulnerable before him in prayer and repentance, are unlikely to be healed. But as people grow in their faith, trust, love and dependence on God, healing inevitably flows into their lives—spiritual healing at first, but physical and emotional healing as well.

* * *

In summary, we have seen how God desires to love us, and how sin keeps us from his love. But though our condition is desperate, it turns out to be curable. God has opened the way for our salvation and healing through Jesus. His blood is sufficient to cleanse us, and his resurrection has power to change us. Through repentance and faith we appropriate these realities. When sin and its consequences are broken in this way, tremendous healing takes place, and new freedom, joy and obedience come to us. We experience anew the presence and reality of God. The truth of his love breaks in again.

We end where we began, with God's desire that his name be known in all the earth and that we delight and glory in "the compassionate and gracious God . . . abounding in love and faithfulness" (Ex 34:6-7). The theological underpinnings for inner healing prayer are to be found in the character, mind and purposes of God—especially as revealed in the person and work of Jesus Christ—and the way he plans for us to live in fellowship with himself and one another. In his death, Jesus took upon himself our sins, weaknesses and diseases and won the right to bear the consequences of all the sin we and others have sown. We are liberated from the cycles of sin and the inevitability of sin and its consequences—including emotional damage and trauma from the past, which can be released by the power of the Holy Spirit through inner healing prayer.

In Jesus we clearly see that God's purpose and desire is to bring healing to us in all dimensions of our lives. God's gift of salvation is for spiritual, physical and emotional healing—God's shalom.

4

USING THE BIBLE IN INNER HEALING

Search me O God and know my heart,
Try me and know my anxious thoughts.
And see if there be any hurtful way in me
And lead me in the everlasting way.

For me (Doug), this simple praise song, based on the last verses in Psalm 139, has become a cry from the heart of Scripture for the reality of inner healing. Our hearts have been broken and hurt by things that have happened to us. These hurts affect us in the present, in the form of anxious thoughts, bad memories and hurtful or wounded emotions. These in turn lead us into various forms of sin, depression, compulsive behaviors, feelings of worthlessness and inferiority, unreasonable fears and anxieties, and so forth.

But our gracious Lord knows us and searches our hearts and is familiar with all our ways (Ps 139:1-3). He is with us always, guiding and holding us in his strong arms (vv. 7-11). He restores our souls and heals us in our inward parts. Our identity is in him, because he has made us fearfully and wonderfully. So we can cry with the psalmist:

For you created my inmost being;
> you knit me together in my mother's womb.

I praise you because I am fearfully and wonderfully made;
> your works are wonderful,
> I know that full well.

My frame was not hidden from you
> when I was made in the secret place.

When I was woven together in the depths of the earth,
> your eyes saw my unformed body.

All the days ordained for me
> were written in your book before one of them came to be.
> (vv. 13-16)

He has made us, and we are his. He searches us, knows our hearts and anxious thoughts, sees the hurtful things that hold us back from him and, through prayer and the power of the Holy Spirit, brings healing and relief as he leads us in the everlasting way.

Emily's Story

I met Emily at a summer training conference. She was well organized, competent, efficient and highly regarded by her colleagues and supervisors. But she had a desperate need to be right, to say the right things, to never make a mistake. As we talked, Emily risked sharing some deep pain and shame from her past.

At age eight, during a monthlong stay at summer camp, Emily became a "special friend" to an older male camp counselor, who would come at night, put a blanket around her bunk and then climb in with her and tell her what he wanted her to do. Emily desperately wanted to be special, as the male counselor told her she was, and so she cooperated with him. He passed information about Emily on to counselors the next summer, and they to others, so that the sexual abuse continued with new counselors during the next four summers. Shame, humiliation, despair, distrust and self-hatred took root in Emily's heart, and these drove the perfectionism that was plaguing her now as an adult.

With Emily's permission, I gathered a team and we prayed together, encouraging her to trust Jesus to be present with her during those hurtful events from her past. She was afraid that Jesus would not want to be there with her, that he would be repulsed and reject her, that he would increase her shame. We prayed for God's peace and loving presence, and gradually Emily was able to relax and sense that Jesus was there, that he saw everything that had happened and that he was not repulsed but was filled with sorrow.

A member of our prayer team received a word of knowledge, a visual image in her mind, that Jesus was kneeling by the bed in that camp dorm room and praying for Emily, interceding for her with tears and groans and agony too deep for words. As this word of knowledge was shared, Emily began to weep. She had learned not to trust people, especially men, but she did trust the Word of God, and she had become an excellent student and interpreter of Scripture. The day before our prayer session, she had been reading in Hebrews that Jesus is at the right hand of the Father making intercession for the saints, and that he "is able to save completely those who come to God through him, because he always lives to intercede for them" (Heb 7:25). This verse had lit up for Emily at the time like a neon sign. Now, a day later, because of her trust and confidence in Scripture, Emily could receive the truth that Jesus was indeed interceding for her. Here was "proof" for her that God did love and accept her and that she could and should forgive herself.

As we read together the affirming and encouraging words of Psalm 139, Emily began to see herself the way God sees her, to agree with him about her value and worth, and to receive his healing power and presence: "You created my inmost being; you knit me together. . . . I am fearfully and wonderfully made."

Emily was on her way to freedom from the damage of sexual abuse.

Through inner healing prayer, the pain anchored in past memories was removed and lost its negative impact. Through the power of God's Word, Emily now saw Jesus present in her past experiences of abuse, praying and interceding for her, loving and forgiving her.

Emily's story shows how important Scripture is in bringing inner healing. But what is the full role, purpose and importance of the Bible for inner healing prayer? Can we operate in the ministry of inner healing with firm confidence that it is supported by God's Word? And how can we use Scripture in inner healing prayer to make sure our ministry remains biblically based?

The Importance of the Bible in Inner Healing

The Bible is critical in the ministry of inner healing prayer. First, those ministering inner healing to others need the confidence that comes from knowing they are praying according to biblical principles and truth. In chapter three we saw that the Bible is our source and guide regarding God's character, the nature of our problems, God's solution in Jesus Christ and his desire to heal our sins and weaknesses. So when we pray for others, we want to be certain we are praying for the problems and issues that God is addressing and that we are working with him toward his purposes.

Second, those we pray for and train need confidence that we are ministering from a strong scriptural base. Those who are familiar with the Bible but have little awareness of God's healing power, or who are wary of seeking power for healing, will gain confidence as they see the biblical principles and foundations behind inner healing prayer.

Because we live in a visually oriented culture, we need to take extra care in praying for people to be sure the images and pictures of God at work come from Scripture and are tested by Scripture. Any representation of God is ultimately idolatrous unless it is something that God has actually given. Scripture is our guard. We will have more to say about the dangers of visualization in chapter eleven.

Third, those who are not familiar with Scripture need to be protected from excesses or mistakes. They deserve biblical explanations for what is happening, so they will not assume we are operating in our own power and ideas and so they will not emulate anything that opposes God's Word and Spirit.

Fourth, the use of Scripture during a prayer session gives people specific verses to use as a "sword of the Spirit" against future doubts and attacks from the enemy. When Emily was tempted to agree with thoughts and inner voices that rose up to accuse her of shame and worthlessness, she could counter with the strong words and images of Scripture that Jesus was present with her, praying for her and delighting in his creation. Scripture provided an unassailable fortress of truth from which Emily could battle the lies and deceits that the enemy had hooked on her past shame. She knew, from the Word, that she was "accepted in the beloved" (Eph 1:6 KJV) and that "there is now no condemnation for those who are in Christ Jesus" (Rom 8:1).

What the Bible Does *Not* Give Us

Nowhere in the Bible do we find the command "Go and do inner ᵣealing!" Phrases like *healing of memories* and *healing of damaged emotions* do not appear in Scripture. Such word descriptions are extrapolated from Scripture; they parallel the word *Trinity* which never appears in the Bible but refers to the biblical reality of One God as Father, Son and Holy Spirit.

Inner healing is a contemporary variety of the Spirit-directed ministries of prayer and counseling that have been practiced in various ways throughout the history of the church. Yet we do not find detailed models, methods or techniques of inner healing prayer in Scripture. To look for detailed models of inner healing in the Bible is like looking for a sample church budget in Paul's letters. Paul has much to say to the churches about money, but we must form our budgets on the basis of truths and principles he gives rather than looking for detailed replicas of our situations. In the same way we must let the Bible inform, shape and direct our practice of prayer ministry in the church.

While Scripture does not include all the terms for inner healing that are currently in use, or step-by-step procedures for inner healing prayer, we do find that every part of the Bible provides foundational support for the reality and need of emotional or inner healing. Jesus, quoting from Deuteronomy, says that God's greatest command is to "love the Lord your God with all your heart and with all your soul and with all your mind" (Mt 22:37)—that is, to love him with our whole being. To effectively love God with our whole being, we need to be free from hurtful memories and from the wounded emotions that lead us into sin, depression, feelings of worthlessness, inferiority, shame and fear. It would seem that God's greatest command for us entails deep emotional and spiritual healing.

What the Bible Does Give Us

The Bible gives us assurance that God is interested in healing our emotions. We have already seen in chapter three that God desires our healing. God knows what is hidden in darkness (Ps 139:11-12; Dan 2:22) and what comes out of the human heart and soul (Mk 7:21-23). His desire is to "wipe away the tears from all faces," to "remove the disgrace of his people from all the earth" (Is 25:8). He sent Jesus to "bind up the brokenhearted" (Is 61:1; Lk 4:18). As one "familiar with suffering," Jesus "took up our infirmities and carried our sorrows" (Is 53:3-4); he gave his life as a ransom for us that we might be whole and at one with the Father. When we seek the Lord, the promise is that he will deliver us from all our fears (Ps 34:4). Paul instructs, even commands, that we "have no anxiety about anything, but in everything by prayer and supplication with thanksgiving let your requests be made known to God" (Phil 4:6 RSV).

It stands to reason that God would provide the means, by his Spirit, to fulfill his promises and commands and bring his will to completion. As the Spirit guides us in prayer for ourselves and others, we receive healing of the soul—heart, mind and emotions.

God's desire to heal our emotions is made clearest in the life and ministry of Jesus. Numerous times in the Gospels, as I noted in chapter three, Jesus deals with lepers and others who were considered sinful, unclean, outcast. Lepers were commanded to make their presence known by shouting "Unclean!" when others were nearby. Surely the emotional scars of leprosy were as severe as the physical scars. Lepers, and others considered unclean, endured abandonment, rejection, hatred, anger, mockery and abuse. They must have suffered self-hatred, poor self-image, despair and anger toward God and others.

Jesus understands the need for physical healing *and* for deep inner healing, for he touched, affirmed and healed lepers, and then instructed them to have their healing certified by the priests so they could return whole to society (Mk 1:40-45). In Luke 17 one healed leper among ten returns to Jesus to give thanks for his healing and to praise God; this shows that he has received healing beyond the physical. Jesus says to him, "Rise and go; your faith has made you well" (v. 19). The purpose of physical and emotional healing is not just that we feel better but that we enter into a lifelong relation with Jesus, who has power to change our lives in every dimension.

As Jesus traveled to heal Jairus's daughter, who lay gravely ill, he was seen by "a woman . . . who had been subject to bleeding for twelve years. She had suffered a great deal under the care of many doctors and had spent all she had, yet instead of getting better she grew worse" (Mk 5:25-26). This woman, who would be considered unclean as long as the flow of blood continued, must have suffered terrible emotional trauma of isolation, anger, rejection, mockery and despair, along with her medical and economic difficulties. In a remarkable act of faith, she dared touch Jesus' garment in the anonymity of a crowded street, and she felt the hemorrhage cease. She was healed of her condition, but more healing was yet to come.

Why did Jesus stop in the midst of a life-and-death situation to speak to this woman? He saw, or knew from his Father, the woman's need for fuller healing. There, in the presence of the whole crowd—many of whom must have been complaining about the delay and wondering why he was bothering with this woman—Jesus gave her his complete attention. First he listened to her whole story, "the whole truth" of what had happened (v. 33), receiving her touch and affirming her as a person loved by God. Second, he explained to her why she had gotten better— "Daughter, your faith has healed you" (v. 34). Jesus must have wanted to clarify for her that it was not magic that made her well. It was not her own strength, nor was it Jesus' cloak. He pointed her to God and the healing power that flowed as a result of her faithful dependence on him.

Finally, in healing her and affirming her, Jesus restored her to society and broke the bonds of isolation, financial worry, abuse from physicians, and the despair and hopelessness associated with the disease. "Go in peace," Jesus said, "and be freed from your suffering" (v. 34).

In the Bible, then, we have assurance that God is interested in healing our spirits, bodies and emotions.

The Bible shows us that sin harms our inner being but that repentance brings healing to the emotions. "Praise the LORD, O my soul," cries David to the One who forgives all our sins and heals all our diseases (Ps 103:1-2). But our thoughts and feelings are torn by trouble. "My guilt has overwhelmed me like a burden too heavy to bear. . . . I am feeble and utterly crushed; I groan in anguish of heart" (Ps 38:4, 8). "For day and night your hand was heavy upon me; my strength was sapped as in the heat of summer. Then I acknowledged my sin to you and did not cover up my iniquity" (Ps 32:4-5).

Zacchaeus, before his encounter with Jesus on the road leading into Jericho, was probably burdened with guilt and groaning in anguish of heart. As a rich tax collector working for the Roman government, he was hated by his fellow Jews and isolated from friends, from the religious community and from his cultural heritage. In his pain and loneliness, he heard stories about a teacher named Jesus who was eating and spending time with tax collectors, sinners and outcasts like Zacchaeus. Perhaps here, he hoped, was someone who could accept him.

Luke 19 tells how, in his eager desire to see Jesus, Zacchaeus took the risk of exposing himself. Then, in a moment of stunning truth, Jesus called him down from the tree and asked to stay at his house! Zacchaeus repented of his sin, and Jesus restored him to his religious and cultural heritage, calling him "a son of Abraham" (v. 9). The guilt and anguish were overcome as "salvation" came to Zacchaeus's house. Then Jesus declared that his purpose and mission were to seek and save what had been lost. Zacchaeus had been perishing, and Jesus had sought him out in order to deliver him and make him whole.

By radically affirming and accepting Zacchaeus in this way—in the midst of a crowd that was murmuring its objections—Jesus powerfully restored Zacchaeus's self-image and sense of worth and brought forth from him an astounding repentance: "Look, Lord! Here and now I give half of my possessions to the poor, and if I have cheated anybody out of anything, I will pay back four times the amount" (v. 8).

Repentance brings healing to the soul. When we confess our transgressions to the Lord, he forgives the guilt of our sin (Ps 32:5).

Wash away all my iniquity
  and cleanse me from my sin. . . .
Let me hear joy and gladness;
  let the bones you have crushed rejoice. . . .
Create in me a pure heart, O God. . . .
Restore to me the joy of your salvation
  and grant me a willing spirit, to sustain me. (Ps 51: 2, 8, 10, 12)

The Bible gives us understanding that sin affects our thoughts, emotions and feelings, but repentance and forgiveness bring cleansing and healing.

The Bible gives us many commands that address our physical and emotional well-being. The two great commands, the Ten Commandments and other summaries of the Law in the Scripture all have implications for emotional health and well-being. A few examples should make this clear.

1. "Honor your father and your mother, as the LORD your God has commanded you, so that you may live long and that it may go well with

you" (Deut 5:16; see also Ex 20:12). John and Paula Sandford, pioneers in the ministry of inner healing, call this one of the most important biblical laws for prayer counselors to know and understand.[1] Wherever we honor our parents in our hearts, they say, life will go well for us. And where we judge, rebel against, reject and dishonor our parents, things will go poorly for us.

This does not mean all parents are honorable and to be obeyed in every circumstance. No parent is without sin. To honor parents is not to excuse or gloss over their sin; but to avoid harsh judgment, one must be ready to give due respect and be willing to forgive. Honoring parents sets in motion a spiritual law—comparable to a natural law such as gravity—that works toward emotional well-being.

A colleague and friend of mine was finally willing, in his mid-thirties, to acknowledge that he had unfairly judged and rejected his parents when he was a teenager. When he was reconciled with his parents, he discovered that other areas of his life, especially his relationships with others, began to improve as well.

2. "Do not judge, or you too will be judged. For in the same way you judge others, you will be judged, and with the measure you use, it will be measured to you" (Mt 7:1-2). If we judge someone mercilessly, we cannot have mercy on ourselves in similar circumstances. If we are harsh and critical toward others, they will react in the same way toward us. Thus our judgments on others bring the same judgment upon ourselves.

Many people carry patterns of emotional strain—including physical symptoms—based on impossibly high standards they have set for themselves and others as a result of harsh judgments made against parents in childhood. Many indicators of the need for inner healing are direct results of harsh judgments, bitterness and anger nursed over the years.

Laura, in chapter one, who hated her father so much, had developed critical and judgmental attitudes toward her parents and other adults; this had profoundly affected her ability to have mercy on others and especially on herself. But desperate for help in overcoming sexual sin, she risked believing the scriptural truth that Jesus came to be with the sick, that he was a friend to sinners, that he would be with her even in her sin. To her surprise, Jesus was not judgmental toward her as she had been toward herself. She repented, received Jesus' forgiveness and healing, and then forgave her father and let go of the bitterness she had harbored. Laura thus gained new grounds for mercy toward herself and others—the new measure she used was being measured to her.

3. "Do not be deceived: God cannot be mocked. A man reaps what he sows. The one who sows to please his sinful nature, from that nature will reap destruction" (Gal 6:7-8). In chapter three we saw the frightening consequences of this cycle of sin: how King David's sins of adultery and murder brought a word from the prophet Nathan that death and sexual excess would be present in the family line. Ammon, Absalom and Solomon reaped what was sown and in turn sowed according to their own sinful natures, reaping destruction.

Every sin bears seeds of destruction for our relationship with God, our relationships with others and our own well-being. Our emotional health is dependent on breaking patterns of generational sin through confession, repentance and giving Jesus authority over past events in inner healing prayer.

4. "You made your vow freely to the LORD your God with your own mouth" (Deut 23:23; see also Mt 5:34; Jas 5:12). There is power and authority in what we vow, or swear by, or receive as a pronouncement or curse. Vows should not be made; sometimes a vow needs to be broken before healing can occur.

In praying for Janice, we discovered that a block to her healing was a vow she had made to "never forgive herself" for something she had done as a young teenager. Janice had run away from home, causing grief and worry to her mother. When the police found her, she fabricated a story of kidnap and rape to cover her tracks. Her story unraveled under police questioning, and full of shame, Janice was returned to her family. When Janice saw the pain she had caused her mother—who had stayed awake nights, waiting at the kitchen window, praying and weeping for her lost daughter—she thought nothing she could ever do would be more terrible than what she had done to her mother, and she vowed never to forgive herself. The breaking of this vow and willing reception of God's forgiveness freed Janice to receive emotional healing.

5. "Is not this the kind of fasting I have chosen: to loose the chains of injustice . . . to set the oppressed free . . . to share your food with the hungry? . . . Then . . . your healing will quickly appear" (Is 58:6-8). Obedience to the Lord's will and purpose brings healing. When we spend ourselves in behalf of hungry and homeless people, then light rises in darkness; the Lord guides and strengthens us; we become like a well-watered garden or a spring whose waters never fail (Is 58:9-11).

There are many more commands we could fruitfully examine: to forgive others so we can be forgiven by our heavenly Father; to love our enemies and pray for those who persecute us; to avoid anger and anxiety. All of these are means by which God encourages our spiritual and emotional health. If we fear the Lord and turn away from evil, he promises to bring health to our bodies and nourishment to our bones (Prov 3:7-8).

The Bible reveals that the enemy wars against our spirits and emotions. Satan is the author of sin, and he continues to tempt and attack us in our areas of weakness (Gen 3:1-6). He is described as our "adversary," a constant and relentless opponent against whom we must be self-controlled and alert: "Your enemy the devil prowls around like a roaring lion looking for someone to devour. Resist him, standing firm in the faith" (1 Pet 5:8-9; see also Zech 3:1). We need to understand how Satan attacks so that we can marshal the defenses God has given us.

Devil means "slanderer." Satan likes nothing better than to distort, defame and slander God's people. Jesus calls him a murderer and liar in whom there is no truth (Jn 8:44). Part of Satan's strategy is to tempt and attack us in our minds and emotions, "sifting" us to find areas of sin or weakness that stem from brokenness or past emotional hurts (Lk 22:31; see also 2 Cor 12:7).

The enemy sifts us in areas of our sinful desires—hatred, quarreling, jealousy, envy, strife, division, selfish ambition (Gal 5:20-21). Such "fruit of the flesh" come out of our past experience, our sinful choices and especially our *responses* to the things that have happened to us. But the strongest attacks often come where memories associated with sin (our own or others') have been suppressed or denied. These can be brought to consciousness by the Holy Spirit through prayer in such a way that the enemy's attack is blocked and inner healing is accomplished. For example, a person who was victimized as a child can be encouraged to understand what happened, express appropriate anger and bitterness, and then confess sins of hatred toward the abuser and bitterness toward God for letting such a thing happen. Inner healing prayer is one means by which such hurts are brought to the surface, healed and removed so that Satan can no longer use them to torment us.

Satan also causes sickness and suffering. Jesus, anointed "with the Holy Spirit and power, . . . went around doing good and healing all who were under the power of the devil, because God was with him" (Acts 10:38). One sabbath day Jesus healed a woman "whom Satan [had] kept bound for eighteen long years" (Lk 13:16).

The enemy seeks to take away the Word of God from our understanding (Mk 4:15) and undermine our trust and confidence in God. His tools and weapons are fear, anxiety and questions about the goodness and faithfulness of God. Adam and Eve were tempted to doubt the Word and the goodness of God. Peter questioned Jesus' word about the purpose of his ministry. Our broken hearts and bent lives can be strengthened and straightened only as we draw close to our loving God. But hatred, fear, anger and anxiety—all signs of our desire to establish our own worth and secure our own future apart from God—keep us from the loving protection he provides, thus opening us to Satan's attacks. "Get behind me, Satan!" Jesus rebukes Peter. "You do not have in mind the things of God, but the things of men" (Mt 16:23).

Satan is our accuser, condemning us before God.

Then I heard a loud voice in heaven say:

"Now have come the salvation and the power and the
kingdom of our God,

and the authority of his Christ.

For the accuser of our brothers,

who accuses them before our God day and night,

has been hurled down." (Rev 12:10)

Satan wants to condemn us and shame us and keep us from knowing what to do about sin. This is the opposite of the conviction of sin that comes from the Holy Spirit, which draws us to confession and repentance and shows us that through Jesus' shed blood there is healing, forgiveness and cleansing.

Accusation, condemnation and shame are favorite weapons of the enemy to cripple us. Self-condemnation, especially, is a frequent cause of inner hurt. In the face of our self-condemnation, Scripture says: "If our heart condemn us, God is greater than our hearts, and knoweth all things" (1 Jn 3:21 KJV). "There is now no condemnation for those who are in Christ Jesus" (Rom 8:1). Satan would like to encourage our shame, for it stands guard at the door of our hearts to keep secret sin hidden away from the light of day. When we are able to confess our sins, the power of shame is broken and we are able to receive the healing and cleansing that God has for us.

The sinful woman (probably a prostitute) in Luke's Gospel, who crashed a party to be with Jesus, surely had to struggle with her own shame as well as the enemy's accusation and condemnation. In the presence of religious leaders and other "proper" people of the day, she stood behind Jesus, weeping, and "began to wet his feet with her tears. Then she wiped them with her hair, kissed them and poured perfume on them" (Lk 7:37-38).

Here is a wonderful picture of shamelessness!

In loving and receiving her, and allowing her to anoint him, Jesus heals her shame. She no longer has the identity of a prostitute, because in the presence of Jesus she can see herself as he sees her. She has a chance to choose again, to have her God-given image restored. Then Jesus explains to the dinner guests that those who know their brokenness and sin and need for forgiveness are able to love most deeply. "She loved much. But he who has been forgiven little loves little" (v. 47).

Jesus came as physician—healer of the human spirit, body and emotions. The religious leaders of his day did not know their own sin and brokenness, and therefore they did not know their need for forgiveness and healing. But this woman knew how much sin, shame and brokenness had been overcome; her gratitude and love overwhelmed any sense of impropriety, embarrassment and fear of shame inherent in her approach to Jesus.

Jesus has brought this woman to a place where full healing can occur—personally and corporately. With her sins forgiven (v. 48), she can be restored to a place in the community. She has been lost, but now she is found. Her self-image and self-esteem are restored; her identity is now centered in Jesus' love. Shame is broken. Love is released.

The Bible reveals that the enemy wars against our spirits and souls, but the power and presence of Jesus bring healing to the whole person.

Biblical Examples of Inner Healing

Many of the psalms richly reveal the patterns and processes of inner healing. "Search me, O God, and know my heart; test me and know my anxious thoughts" (139:23). David cries out for God to know the secret sin of his heart, to see the hurtful and broken things that need repair and healing, and then to lead him into wholeness and salvation—"the way everlasting" (139:24). In Psalm 103 David reminds his own soul—heart, mind and emotions—to "praise the LORD . . . and forget not all his benefits": forgiveness, healing from all disease, lifting him from darkness and despair, giving him love and mercy, satisfying him with a lifetime of good things, constantly renewing his whole being (vv. 2-5). Psalm 51 is a model for self-examination and inner renewal. In these and other psalms we are immersed deeply in the biblical call and promise for healing of the inner person.

Biblical stories, too, show us how reinterpreting a past hurtful event can bring freedom and healing from the pain of its memory. Joseph was treated shamefully by his brothers. They plotted to kill him, stripped him of his clothes, threw him in an abandoned well and then sold him into slavery. But later Joseph was able to reinterpret his brothers' betrayal in light of the purposes of God: "So then, it was not you who sent me here, but God" (Gen 45:8). And later he says to his brothers, "Don't be afraid. Am I in the place of God? You intended to harm me, but God intended it for good to accomplish what is now being done, the saving of many lives" (Gen 50:19-20). Seeing God's purpose and plan being worked out through his loss and suffering has freed Joseph from bitterness, anger and need for revenge.

In Luke 24:13-35, the disciples on the way to Emmaus are hurt and disillusioned in the wake of Jesus' crucifixion. Using the Scriptures, however, Jesus reinterprets their negative experience into a fundamentally meaningful one, giving them hope, healing and newness of life.

Peter's betrayal of Jesus and final restoration show us how reliving a past episode can bring inner healing. Peter had boasted that he would follow Jesus to prison and to death (Lk 22:33). When Jesus is arrested, Peter follows along to the house of the chief priest, where he watches as Jesus is beaten (Jn 18:22). While warming his hands over a charcoal fire outside the priest's home (Jn 18:18), Peter, fearful and defensive, betrays Jesus three times. Just as he finishes his denial, a rooster crowed. "The Lord turned and looked straight at Peter. Then Peter remembered the word the Lord had spoken to him: 'Before the rooster crows today, you will disown me three times.' And [Peter] went outside and wept bitterly" (Lk 22:61-62). Shame, fear and weakness—exposed by pride, boasting and betrayal—are lodged in Peter's inner being.

Later, after the resurrection, Jesus prepares a meal on the shore for the disciples. When Peter hears that the Lord is there, he hurries to him. The first thing he sees is "a fire of burning coals . . . with fish on it, and some bread" (Jn 21:9). Surely the smell of this charcoal fire reminded Peter vividly of the scene of his betrayal of Jesus. (In all of the New Testament, this Greek word for "charcoal fire" appears only in these two texts.)

At the end of the meal, three times Jesus asks Peter, "Do you truly love me?" (Jn 21:15-17). The three questions unlock the bondage of the three betrayals as Jesus heals Peter and restores him to ministry, charging him to "feed my sheep." Inner healing comes as Peter is restored through reliving the hurtful event. Peter thus learns a lesson he will never forget, a depth of humility he probably could not have learned in any other way. Though the enemy "sifted" Peter (Lk 22:31-32) and tempted him at a point of weakness, God overcomes and triumphs even through Peter's fall.

Later, filled with the Spirit, Peter boldly proclaims the truth of Jesus as the Son of God before the Sanhedrin—the rulers, elders and teachers of the law, the very people in whose shadow he had betrayed his Lord.

There are numerous biblical examples of people being lost—in sin, brokenness, separation from others, separation from God—and being found, restored in self-image and worth to themselves, families, culture and God. We have looked at the woman in Luke 7 whose shame is broken and whose God-given self-image is restored. She was lost and is found. Other examples abound—the woman with the flow of blood, lepers, those possessed of demons or declared unclean or unacceptable.

Perhaps the most celebrated example of one being separated, lost, found and restored is the story of the prodigal son. Jesus gives us a wondrous picture of our loving Father-God in the person of the prodigal's father, who acts contrary to cultural expectations in restoring his wayward but repentant son to a place of importance in the family. The father gives a ring and a robe, restores self-esteem and sense of value and worth, expresses his gladness and shows his love. This parable reveals Jesus' mission and ministry to seek out the lost, those in whom the image of God has been marred or distorted. It reveals God's love for us, his desire to heal, renew and restore our inner person.

The Bible gives us assurance that God is interested in healing; that while sin damages us, repentance brings healing to our spirits, minds and emotions; that God's commands are directed to our spiritual and emotional well-being; that the enemy's strategy is to weaken our emotional health; and that inner healing happens in the presence of Jesus and under the covering of the Father's love and mercy. In fact, the Bible gives us a solid foundation for inner healing prayer.

Scripture in the Inner Healing Process

Here let's explore how using the Bible at key points during prayer keeps our ministry biblically based.[2]

A longer passage of Scripture can provide a framework for inner healing. Psalm 139, for example, declares that God knows us intimately and has always been present with us, even before birth. When you are praying through a difficult past event in someone's life, or when a traumatic experience is suddenly brought to memory, it is critical to acknowledge that God was there, knows everything that happened, cares about the person and is able to act sovereignly through the event to bring healing and mercy. When people realize that God was present, loving them and identifying with them, they can trust him in new ways. Forgiveness and repentance become easier, and they gain new faith and confidence that God will be present in the future as well.

So you might ask the person you are praying for to read Psalm 139 through with you, looking and listening for themes that God may want to raise for inner healing. If the person needs healing from some past event, read verses 7-12 aloud as he or she listens prayerfully. Then help the person to ask God how he was present during the event, and proceed according to what God reveals.[3]

When the person's own sin is the critical issue, verses 11-12 are especially helpful. No "darkness" can hide us from God. Hearing this word from God often brings conviction of sin and leads to confession and forgiveness.

For people with low self-esteem, the psalm tells how God lovingly formed them in their mother's womb, how wonderfully they are made, and how God is constantly thinking of them and declaring them to be special. Have them reread verses 13-18, and ask whether they believe this about themselves. It may be helpful to pray through their experience in the womb, acknowledging that God purposed them, desired them, delighted in them. We need to be able to agree with the psalmist in praising God for the way he has made us—"fearfully and wonderfully"—including our bodies, minds and personalities. It can be helpful to read verses 13-16 aloud, inserting the name of the one being prayed for: "We praise you because Maria is fearfully and wonderfully made; your works—especially Maria—are wonderful, we know that full well."

Anger may arise during such a prayer. Verses 19-22 can encourage us to pray our anger as the psalmist did. This opens the anger to God so that it is no longer locked inside. After praying his anger, the psalmist asks God to search his heart for wickedness. This can encourage openness for prayer about unforgiveness and bitterness.

At the end of a prayer session, returning to verses 1-4 can be a wonderful reminder of how close God is, how he knows everything about us—when we sit down and stand, all our thoughts and ways, the concerns that are on our minds—and because he knows us so intimately we can bring everything to him and enter into the intimacy he desires with us. He sees the hurtful things that hold us back and brings healing and relief as he leads us in the everlasting way (vv. 23-24).

Psalm 139 provides a helpful starting point for God's work of inner healing by focusing us on his presence and his love. For people who may be nervous about receiving guidance from God during prayer, or who are just beginning to open their emotions to God, this text provides the best framework for a first experience of listening to God and being guided by the Holy Spirit.

At times we may need to use Scripture to interpret and explain our prayers. It is helpful to have scriptural support to show why we are praying in certain ways. For example, I prayed for Larry, a young man at Urbana 90, about habits and shame from past sexual involvements which were causing him difficulty in his new marriage. Sensing that we needed to break the bonds that had been established in previous sexual relationships, I reviewed with Larry the concept of sexual bonding from 1 Corinthians 6:15-20, where Paul speaks about uniting with prostitutes. Larry wanted to have these bonds broken and was willing to repent and ask God's forgiveness for his behavior toward several women. We then had an extended prayer time as the Holy Spirit guided Larry to specific bonds that needed to be broken and specific acts of sin that needed to be confessed.

Afterward we shared our impressions about the time of prayer. Larry expressed gratitude for the Scripture passage, for it had helped him understand and had bolstered his faith. He could take this passage home with him as a "sword of the Spirit" to strengthen his faith in times of struggle.

Here is a beginning list of Scripture passages that are helpful for inner healing prayer sessions. You may wish to copy them in your Bible for easy reference.

God's love: Is 43:1-7 (I love you), Ex 34 (abounding in steadfast love), John 3:16 (God so loved . . .), Rom 8:31-39 (nothing can separate us from the love of God), Eph 3:17-19 (the love of Christ surpasses knowledge)

God's intention to free us: Lk 4:18-19 (free the captives)

God's providence: Gen 50:20 (about Joseph), Rom 8:28 (in all things God is working for the good)

Christ's lordship over all: Col 1:15-18 (in him all things are created and held together), Phil 2:9-11 (Jesus is Lord)

Christ's empathy with our pain: Heb 4:14-16 (tempted as we are), Mk 14:32-42 (agony in Gethsemane), passion narratives

Generational sin: Ex 34:7 and Deut 5:9 (to the third and fourth generations), Ex 20:12 (honor your parents)

Confession: Dan 2:22 (God sees what is in darkness), 1 Jn 1:5-9 (if we confess our sins he will forgive us), Jas 5:16 (confess your sins . . . pray . . . be healed)

The cross: Rom 8:1-4 (no condemnation because of Jesus' sacrifice), Col 1:19-23 (we are reconciled through his death), Col 2:15 (in the cross Jesus triumphed over the principalities and powers), 1 Jn. 2:1-2 (he is the expiation for our sins)

God's forgiveness: John 8:1-12 (the adulterous woman), 1 Jn 1:9 (if we confess our sins he will forgive us), 1 Jn 3:19-20 (when our hearts condemn us)

Forgiving others: Mt 6:12 (the Lord's Prayer), Mt 6:14-15 (forgiving and being forgiven), Mt 18:21-35 (the law of forgiveness—unforgiving servant)

Judgment: Mt 7:1-2 (do not judge or you too will be judged)

Sexual bonding: 1 Cor 6:15-20 (your body is the temple of the Holy Spirit)

Putting sin to death: Col 3:5 (put to death what is earthly), Gal 2:20 (I have been crucified with Christ)

The effectiveness of prayer: Jer 29:13 (seeking with all our hearts), Mt 18:20 (where two or three are gathered), Lk 11:5-13 (ask, seek, knock—receive), Heb 4:16 (drawing near to the throne of grace)

The Holy Spirit praying for us: Rom 8:26-27 (the Spirit intercedes for us)

Our authority in prayer: Mt 16:19, 18:18 (binding and loosing), Jn 20:23 (if you forgive the sins of any, they are forgiven)

Spiritual armor: Eph 6:10-18 (the armor of God)

Submitting the will: Eph 4:21-32 (be subject out of reverence), Jn 5:6 (do you want to be healed?)

"All Scripture is God-breathed and is useful for teaching, rebuking, correcting and training in righteousness" (2 Tim 3:16). In the midst of a prayer session, the Holy Spirit will often bring to mind a Scripture verse or reference that confirms what is happening or sets the direction for what is to happen. The Holy Spirit often teaches and corrects in this way when a person has doubts about what God is like or persistent wrong ideas about God. And when someone is ready to take a crucial step of faith, a command or promise from the Word can be very significant.

Mei-ling was unsure of God's love and afraid that he would not want to be with her if we asked Jesus to be present. As we prayed against fear and asked for strength and courage for Mei-ling, she said the refrain of a song kept running through her mind, with the words "something new I will do." At the same time a member of our prayer group received the word "Isaiah 43." Two team members began softly singing a praise song based on portions of Isaiah 43, including these words:

Truly now I will do something new.
Soon it will come to light, then will you know it.
I will find a way, rivers in the wasteland,
Open the desert streams, something new I will do.

Do not fear, for now you are redeemed
I have called your name and I love you.

These words became a lullaby from Jesus to Mei-ling as he drew close to her and she received the assurance of his presence and his love. Before the song was finished, Jesus had hugged Mei-ling, held her close, played with her in a grassy field like a big brother and showed her that he was filling her heart with love. Together they watched a "love-o-meter" in her heart rise from empty to full—confirming the scriptural promise that God had called Mei-ling's name and he loved her.

In another prayer session, Richard, who struggled with anger and self-hatred and fears of being unwanted by his adoptive parents (who had abused him), remarked that the words "Psalm 68 verse 4" were echoing in his mind. We opened the Bible and read: "Sing to God, sing praise to his name. . . . A father to the fatherless, a defender of widows, is God in his holy dwelling. God sets the lonely in families, he leads forth the prisoners with singing" (Ps 68:4-6). These comforting words from Scripture enabled Richard to take the next steps in trusting God for healing.

It is helpful to keep a journal or notes in your Bible of the ways God guides you in prayer through the Scripture. You can use these records as testimony to others, as swords of the Spirit to thwart attacks from the enemy, and as helps for praying with others. The more Scripture we have appropriated, digested and memorized, the more available we are to God, for we become channels of his healing word and presence.

People of the Word

Our challenge is to be ever more deeply a people of the Word. The authority of Scripture is a central dynamic in inner healing prayer. The Bible must be our foundation and guide as we pray for those who have been deeply wounded.

In answer to the questions posed at the beginning of this chapter, we have seen that we can enter into prayer for inner healing with firm confidence that it is supported by God's Word. We can rely on Scripture to guide us in our prayers, ensuring a biblical basis—and continuing correction—for our ministry of inner healing.

As we enter faithfully into such prayer, we will be guided by the Holy Spirit to discover new meaning and application in familiar scriptural texts. We will find that Scripture saves us from unwise practices and gives us confirmation, inspiration and correction. And we will be challenged to minister in deeper and more expectant ways.

Scripture will come alive for us just as it did for Emily, who saw that Jesus was interceding for *her,* that God did love and accept her and that she could and should forgive herself. God promises that profound inner change awaits those who seek him and are open to his Word and power. To the Sadducees Jesus said: "You are in error because you do not know the Scriptures or the power of God" (Mt 22:29). Let's not be Sadducees. Let's pray with the authority of Scripture and the power of the Holy Spirit.

Scriptural authority is a first and most important principle of inner healing prayer. In the next two chapters we review additional principles for an effective ministry of inner healing—dynamics having to do with the authority and the love of God.

5

JESUS'
HEALING
AUTHORITY

Jesus, *how are you praying for Dennis?"* one of the prayer team asked. As we listened, I (Doug) had a picture of Jesus standing by a park bench while Dennis went running by him at top speed—so fast that he was a blur.

Without voicing this impression, I asked Dennis how he was feeling. He poured out a litany of anxiety—about what vocation he should choose, what college major would best prepare him for this vocation, whether he should continue to date his current girlfriend, and what he should do with the rest of his life. He wanted immediate answers to all these questions. He had been praying for God's guidance but did not trust any of the ideas that came to his mind. He spoke rapidly and almost shook with tension.

"Slow down," I said to him. "Dennis, you are so consumed with anxiety you aren't giving God time or room to give you guidance. You are giving more authority to anxiety than you are to Jesus. Can you relax enough to let Jesus be with you? I think he wants to show you something. I had a picture of Jesus standing by a park bench, waiting. Let's see if he will give you the same picture."

As we continued in prayer, Dennis received an image of Jesus standing by a park bench, and he thought Jesus was showing him a video, but it went by so fast he couldn't see what it was.

"Jesus, could you run it by again?" he asked. Again it was a blur.

"Jesus, could you show it to me one more time?" he pleaded.

"Yes," Jesus spoke to Dennis's spirit; "I'll show it to you one more time in the slowest possible motion." Then Dennis saw himself running by Jesus at top speed without even so much as a sideways glance.

When he shared this with us, we all laughed. What had been obvious to us was now obvious to Dennis. He asked to be forgiven for giving so much authority to anxiety and frantic activity and so little authority and time to Jesus.

And then, as we prayed, he saw Jesus slow him down, sit with him on the bench and say, "I want you to be with me, and I'll be with you if you'll slow down and let me be Lord. I've got great plans for you, but we'll have to take it a day at a time."

*　*　*

Authority is a key dynamic in inner healing. Throughout the Scriptures we see God proclaiming, establishing and defending his authority. When the people of Israel consistently dodged and disregarded his authority, he packed them off into exile for seven decades of pondering and repentance, after which a remnant returned to take up a more obedient relationship with him.

God's authority might be described as "the right to command or expect an obedient response or action." God has authority because he is himself. " 'I AM' is speaking with you" was sufficient self-declaration to move Moses to obedience (Ex 3:14). I AM's Son displayed God's authority in every area of life and modeled for us the relationship between being under authority and having authority. Because Jesus was perfectly obedient to the Father, he had the right to exercise the Father's authority in every way and degree. Jesus has authority to protect us, heal us, forgive us and use us; and we can receive that same authority when we willingly put ourselves under his authority through repentance, renouncing idolatries, exercising faith and walking in obedience.

For Dennis, anxiety had taken the place of Jesus and become an idolatry. Dennis had given God's rightful authority to something other and less than God. God alone can adequately stand in the position of God. When anything else stands in his place, it is as if a carousel were rotating around a pole which is off-center: eventually the whole thing must come apart. Only God can stand the stress of being at the center of things.

We see the authority of Jesus in inner healing (1) when things that compete with his lordship are revealed and broken through repentance, (2) when he reframes and heals hurtful memories and (3) when healing comes as he is present in past events. Let's look at these three dynamics.

Jesus' Lordship

Jesus opened the Great Commission by claiming. "All authority in heaven and on earth has been given to me" (Mt 28:18). Through the cross Jesus won the right to be Lord and master of our lives; by his loving self-sacrifice he proved that he deserves our trust, confidence and allegiance. No matter what happens to us in life, Jesus has authority to overcome its negative effects. This is a key principle in inner healing because we often discover, even in committed Christians, that some element such as worry, fear, anger or self-condemnation can be given more authority in certain realms of life than Jesus.

In the midst of a weeklong conference, an early-morning phone call from the conference administrator told me that one participant, a man named Bob, could not get out of bed because of extreme pain in his back. "Would you go and pray for him?" the administrator pleaded.

As I walked down the hallway toward Bob's room, I noticed a sharp pain in my own upper back, just under the left shoulder blade. I sensed that this pain might have been given by the Spirit in sympathy with Bob, as an indication of God's readiness to heal. As I interviewed Bob and determined that the pain in his back was indeed under the left shoulder blade, my faith was quickened to see God at work in healing. I prayed with Bob and his wife, and we took authority over the pain and then waited on God for guidance.

After a moment, I asked God if there was any root or cause for this pain, and a strong impression of "worry" came to my mind. I began to pray against worry, and the Spirit seemed to be saying that the worry had to do with finances. I stopped for a moment and asked Bob and his wife if they were struggling with financial worries.

As they told a lengthy tale of financial woes and concern, they began to realize that they had fallen into a deep distrust of God and had been unable to believe that he would care for them in their current circumstances. They were actually giving more authority to fear and worry than they were to Jesus.

As they repented, the pain in my back faded, and within minutes Bob too was feeling much better. We closed with thanksgiving to God. Later they reported that in the following hour they shared a wonderful prayer time during which God showed them patterns and roots of worry and fear going back into their individual pasts, and they were able to give these over to God. Bob's soreness was completely gone in twenty-four hours.

Acts of repentance for any idolatry that competes with Jesus' lordship open the door for God's mercy, love and healing power to flow forth. Repentance and renewed confession of faith always strengthen Jesus' authority in our lives.

During prayer for inner healing, we have found that sometimes Jesus will not enter easily into a remembered event or reveal where he was or what he was doing. This is usually a clue that something or someone has been given an authority that blocks the authority of Jesus.

Stacy had always been "Daddy's little girl." Her father was a well-known high-school athletic coach, and she was his cheerleader, eager to please him in every way. When she was fifteen, however, Stacy's parents divorced and her father moved away. She felt angry and abandoned—but also responsible, as though her absence from home during the busy junior-high years had brought about the divorce and the loss of the dad who meant everything to her. During the next four years Stacy abused herself with sex, alcohol and drugs, and her shame and self-hatred grew.

In college Stacy began to follow Jesus and to seek healing and forgiveness for her past sin and self-abuse. One morning I had the opportunity to pray with her. But as we prayed through the painful memories in Stacy's past, Jesus would not come into the memories to show us what was happening. We asked if anything stood in the way or blocked Jesus' authority, and the Spirit revealed to Stacy that her idolization of her father had prevented her from giving complete allegiance to Jesus; she feared that commitment to Jesus would betray her father. As she repented and asked Jesus to have authority, he quickly entered into the memories that needed healing and showed Stacy his love and compassion.

Sin, brokenness, rebellion and faithless reliance on the things of this world for security and protection keep us in bondage, isolated from the protection Jesus affords us by his sacrifice and blood. We are often unaware that we are placing our trust in ourselves or in material things rather than in Christ. We are blinded by false idolatries that compromise our submission and obedience to Jesus.

Mike and I often pray for people who are surprised when the Spirit reveals to them that Jesus is not Lord in specific areas of their lives. As they repent and give him authority in these areas, healing begins to flow.

I prayed at some length recently for Kelly, a graduate student in the humanities who felt no sense of God's present reality or of his love and desire for intimacy with her. The daughter of a pastor, she had been raised in the Christian faith and had been loyal to the traditions and customs of her church. But as a graduate student in a hostile academic environment, she became filled with cynicism and doubts. As we talked

I learned that Kelly had not experienced any close intimacy with her earthly father, that she had a highly developed sense of responsibility for others, and that beginning in high school she had felt "different, on my own, responsible and lonely."

As we asked the Spirit to break through the barriers to Kelly's intimacy with God, Kelly had a memory of sitting alone at the lunch table in high school.

"Could you let Jesus be there with you?" I asked. "He promised to be with us always and has been present to everything that has ever happened to you."

"OK," she responded; then she suddenly reported that Jesus was sitting across the table from her.

"What's he doing?"

"He's just sitting there, not saying or doing anything, as though he is waiting for something."

"I think Jesus wants to come close and perhaps give you a hug," I said. "Is that all right?"

Kelly said yes, and immediately Jesus moved to her side of the table and put his arms around her. She saw herself hugging Jesus back, a rather perfunctory hug lasting only a second or two, and then pushing him away. But Jesus didn't want to let go. "He wants to be with me!" she exclaimed. "He is saying things to me and wants to keep my attention."

Then the picture changed, and Kelly saw a long line of people in front of her with Jesus bringing up the rear, and she was hugging each one as fast as she could.

"Why do I have Jesus at the back of the line?" she asked aloud.

"Do you want him to come to the head of the line? Do you want him to have authority over your relationships and be Lord of everything in your—"

"Yes, I want him to be Lord!" she responded, before I could finish my sentence. Then she saw Jesus come toward her from the end of the line, growing bigger and scooping up all the others in line—including

Kelly—and hugging them all together. He said, "Put me first and everything else will be yours as well. You can love all these people better through me. Will you let me love you, and these people through you?"

Jesus, eager to exert his proper authority in Kelly's life, seized the opportunity afforded by prayer and broke the idolatries and false understandings that had blocked her intimacy with him. He extended his care and protection to her. He gave her the ability to take new initiatives of love with both her parents.

We have found that the enemy often works through shame and fear—even in seemingly mature believers—to cripple and hold people back from the healing and joy that the Lord promises. Shame and fear stand as guards at the door of our past, preventing us from allowing hurts, sins or embarrassments to come to light and be healed. When these things are kept hidden, we are trusting more in secrecy to protect us than the Lord Jesus.

It is the truth that makes us free, for the truth is that no sin is beyond God's forgiveness and, again, "there is now no condemnation for those who are in Christ Jesus" (Rom 8:1). This enables us to rebuke shame and fear and give Jesus permission to overcome them by his blood and strengthen us to receive the fullness of his grace and mercy. His full authority, our acknowledgment of his full lordship, opens the way to healing, growth and maturity in him.

Reframing

Often Jesus exercises authority in inner healing by *reframing* a hurtful event.[1] I (Mike) define reframing as taking another look at an event from a different perspective or through someone else's eyes. As Doug noted in chapter four, we think this is what Jesus was doing for Peter in the resurrection appearance on the banks of the Sea of Galilee. Since he asked three times, "Simon son of John, do you love me?" it's pretty clear that he had Peter's threefold denial in mind. Giving Peter the opportunity to affirm three times that he loved Jesus put his denial in a new light: it brought closure to the denial, it brought healing to Peter's memory of the denial, and it officially counteracted the effects of the denial.

Reframing helps us see an event that hurt us through the Lord's eyes. And how Jesus sees things is how they truly are.

Cindy, a married woman in her mid-thirties, came for counseling because of compulsive fears that she might hurt people. Taking care of children in the church nursery, she would suddenly be seized with fear that she might harm one of them. Or she would be terrified that a cake she had just baked for a church bazaar contained poison. She was sure she had not put poison in it, but the thought wouldn't leave her, and she would worry that someone would die from eating the cake. Cindy lived in considerable fear and insecurity, and she was overly protective of her own young children.

As we prayed for inner healing, the Lord quickly took Cindy to an early childhood experience with her mother at the grocery store. As Cindy and her mom stood waiting in the checkout line, the woman just behind them suddenly collapsed to the floor. Cindy's mom grabbed Cindy, whisked her away and never spoke with her about the incident. But Cindy was haunted by the thought that *she* had caused the woman to fall down and die.[2] This childish sense of omnipotence, of assumed responsibility for the woman's condition, had initiated the pattern of fear.

As we prayed through this childhood memory, Jesus took Cindy by the hand and showed her what had actually happened. The woman had fainted in a heap behind Cindy, but Jesus was there helping the woman to her feet and comforting her. She did not die! Cindy's mother, wanting to protect her little girl, had inadvertently deepened her fear by whisking her away and not talking about what had happened. Now she saw Jesus present in the experience and he reframed it for her, showing her what actually happened and that he was in charge and that all was well. As he said to her, "Don't be afraid," she felt her fear and panic leave. She was on the path to healing from ingrained patterns of fear and insecurity.

Sometimes reframing requires the active collaboration of two or more persons. On one occasion, for example, I (Mike) felt I needed inner healing for a rejection I had received from my wife, who had ignored a bid for intimacy. I kept on saying to myself, "I forgive her," but I continued to smart from her rejection. Finally I decided to follow the advice of Matthew 18 and tell her my concern so that I could express my forgiveness to her directly.

After I explained the hurt, Sue looked at me for a moment with an expression of astonishment. Finally she said, "I wasn't rejecting you, I thought you were joking, and I was just hurrying to get my chores done."

As soon as I realized that she did not *intend* to reject me, my hurt feelings evaporated. This was inner healing by reframing.

Interactions like this are extremely important. One reason the Scriptures tell us to confront those who have offended us is that that's the only way we get to hear their side of it. In such confrontations no one has ever completely agreed with my reading of their behavior. They always see their behavior through their own eyes, which are quite different from mine. And it's only when I ask others about their behavior that I hear an explanation of their intent.

In any interaction between us, I see only my intention while you see only my behavior. If you don't ask me what my intention is, guess what? You supply *your* intention as the motive for *my* behavior and then react to your own intention. I've seen people feud for years without ever checking out their perceptions or simply asking about each other's intentions.

We mentioned Joseph's reframing of his personal tragedy in the last chapter. With amazing economy of thought and speech, he summarized, "You intended to harm me, but God intended it for good" (Gen 50:20). When he first disclosed himself to his terrified brothers, he said, "Do not be distressed and do not be angry with yourselves for selling me here, because it was to save lives that *God* sent me ahead of you" (Gen 45:5). When all was said and done, it became clear to Joseph that it was

God, not his brothers, who had engineered his arrival in Egypt. It was all for a divine purpose.

Our philosophy of divine operations might not square with the idea that God used sinful means to accomplish holy goals. Surely Joseph's brothers sinned against him. Yet God turned it for good. If it was so important to get Joseph into Egypt, why didn't God use a more godly manner of getting him there? Because God delights in turning the devil's actions for his own purposes.

Another and greater deliverance was accomplished in the same manner. It is clear from the Gospels that Satan strategized to accomplish the crucifixion of Jesus. But Peter declared that it was done "by *God's* set purpose and foreknowledge" (Acts 2:23). Satan did his worst to sabotage the plan of God, but God used Satan's efforts to fulfill that very plan. How great is our God! Black Friday became Good Friday! The snake swallowed its own tail!

This is why the followers of Jesus Christ can "count it all joy," can "rejoice in tribulation," can "endure patiently." As Norman Grubb states, "If God's gifts are our blessings, and the devil's assaults are also our blessings, what remains to harm or depress us? If good is good, and evil is equally good to the enlightened, then a realm of life is entered where we rejoice always, in everything give thanks, and in all things are more than conquerors."[3]

This is reframing. This is seeing things from God's perspective. This is loosing the power and authority of God upon the works of the world, the flesh and the devil.

Reaction, an important factor related to reframing, needs to be mentioned here. As we indicated in the first chapter, our reaction largely determines how much an event will hurt us. If a parent in a drunken uproar rejects two children equally, the one who resents the parent will be the one who is hurt; the one who forgives the parent is the one who will not need healing. It's not so much what is done to you but *how you react to it* that determines whether you will be hurt.[4]

This is one reason Jesus emphasized forgiveness so much. "For if you forgive men when they sin against you, your heavenly Father will also forgive you" (Mt 6:14) seems to be the summary statement. The Greek word translated "forgive" has the meaning "to send away, to dismiss." God's command is for all of us to dismiss the sin and guilt of those who have offended us. Not to dismiss their sin is to allow it to work its full negative impact on our hearts and minds. But to send it away seems to prevent that negative effect. It's almost as though a negative event comes into an anteroom of our minds where we either send it right back out the door through forgiveness or refuse to dismiss it and thus usher it on through an inner door to our hearts.

This does not mean that we ignore the procedures for reconciliation Jesus prescribed in Matthew 18 and Luke 17. There are times when we must confront the offender. But we must have already dismissed their offense from *our* heart by the time the confrontation takes place. Not to dismiss it is to allow its negative work to spread. Dismissing the sin from our heart is the best preparation for it to be dismissed from the heart of the other.

Contemporaneity

Normally when we use the word *contemporaneous,* we mean that two people or events occupy the same time frame. In the Western world-view,[5] time is unconsciously seen as linear: we think of time as a line on which past, present and future take their proper positions. We inherited this thought-form from our Greco-Roman forebears. But the Hebrew culture in which the Bible was birthed did not regard time as linear so much as contemporaneous. This is difficult for Westerners to grasp, so stay with me for a moment while I try to explain.

Scholars tell us that the Hebrew language has no past- or present-tense forms of verbs. Instead, actions are classified as either complete or incomplete. When using English, a Jew might well describe yesterday's event in *present-tense* verbs: "And so Marvin and I are going down Fairfax Avenue and we're turning into the deli and Marvin is saying . . ." It's not that the Jew doesn't know that the past exists or that an event is over. Rather, his heritage includes a radically different understanding of time. To put it briefly, contemporaneity means that moments from the past and the present converge on each other. As a wave at the seashore curls over and moves upon the rest of the water, some of which is receding in the opposite direction, so past and present can curl in on each other.

Contemporaneity for the Hebrew is activated by memory. When the father of the Jewish family says at the seder on the day of the Passover, "Thank you for bringing us out of the land of Egypt," a two-directional contemporaneity occurs. The forebears who actually were brought out of Egypt are now mysteriously present. And those assembled around the table are somehow actually making their escape from Egypt in the loins of their forebears. Past and present curl in on each other.[6] That is, they are contemporaneous.

When King David's son Absalom realized that he would have no male heirs, he got a bit panicky, for there would be no "ben-Absalom" to carry his name. This was tragic, for in his culture being remembered was being immortal. The remembered one was somehow mysteriously brought into the present by being recalled. So Absalom did a canny thing: he had an odd-shaped tower built right beside one of the main roads into Jerusalem, knowing that arriving strangers would inquire about it. When the answer came, "Oh, that's Absalom's tower," he would be remembered, and therefore immortal despite his lack of heirs (2 Sam 18:18).

Something of this dynamic was lying behind Jesus' command at the Last Supper, "Do this in remembrance of me" (Lk 22:19). He knew that when the disciples gathered to eat and drink in remembrance of his sacrifice, all the benefits of that sacrifice would be available—present!—for them once again.

This concept is important in inner healing, because it means that Jesus is Lord *over* time, not under time. In other words, he was truly present in the past event in which someone was hurt. His presence can be realized in faith and actualized so that his healing power is released into the memory of the painful event.

Laura, whose story was told in chapter one, rejected her father early in life because of physical and emotional abuse. Remember that we didn't make the mistake of asking Jesus to *change* her personal history, for he is and always has been stronger than history. What we need to do is ask him to *heal* history. So we can say something like "Lord, we ask you to go back in time to the moment when this event occurred," and he actually does so through his lordship over time and his understanding of the contemporaneity of all moments under his lordship.

The arm of the Lord is not shortened. Not even the past is exempt from his authority and power.

When we understand this, our hearts can take flight in ever-widening hope. When I realize Jesus' presence in my past, I know that I am not a captive of my past, that my history is in fact redeemable, that my old life was truly put to death on the cross, that Jesus is victorious even over what lies behind me.

Jesus is Lord—even over time! Thanks be to God.

6

JESUS' HEALING LOVE

Along *with Jesus' powerful authority—over time, past and pres-*
ent sin, hurtful events and ensuing memories—there is a second category of key dynamics in inner healing prayer: the healing love of Jesus.

Love is central to the character of God, who "so loved the world that
he gave his one and only Son, that whoever believes in him shall not
perish but have eternal life" (Jn 3:16). In chapter three we saw that Jesus'
every word and action, his love and compassion for those around him,
are reflections to us of the heart, will and character of God. What Jesus
reveals to us is that God's central loving purpose is to bring salvation,
healing and wholeness to his people.

The strongest command in the New Testament is to "love one another" in the same way that Jesus loves us. Our primary purpose in
praying inner healing for people is to enable them to experience and
receive God's love—to experience the presence and love of Christ him-

self sharing in their fear of abandonment, their lack of human love, the abuse and other traumas they have suffered. Early in chapter one we saw how Jonathan received God's healing presence and love as Jesus was present in his past memories of being fearful and lonely. The presence of Jesus, who played with him in a burned-out army tank, brought healing for Jonathan's pain and loneliness.

The dynamic of love reveals (1) God's heartfelt desire for intimacy with us, (2) the healing power of his forgiveness and (3) the exchange of our sins and weaknesses for his salvation and healing. Let's examine these three dynamics.

Intimacy with God

Paul gives us a wonderful promise in 1 Corinthians 13:8: "Love never fails." Scholars explain that the Greek words carry an emphasis that calls us to keep on keeping on in love, in the faith and hope that it will achieve its ends.

As Mike and I have engaged in inner healing prayer for people over the years, we have found that God's desire for intimacy with his people, and for them to know the deepest levels of intimacy with him, is constant and unfailing. In chapter three I told of praying for a man in Hong Kong, and how the aggressive love of Jesus reached out to draw this man into close intimacy, so much that Jesus took the man's brokenness and sin into his own body. I saw how much God loved this man, who could not read or write, who had been involved in prostitution, drug dealing, gambling—the worst kind of sin and human degradation—and yet who was made in God's image. And I saw by implication how much God loves each one of us. Time and again God has spoken his love into my heart and experience, melting me down and causing me to trust and love him beyond my human abilities and inclinations.

The Scriptures encourage us to let God have all our worries and cares, for he is always thinking about us and watching over us (1 Pet 5:7). Our God is a God of detail. He has numbered the hairs of our heads. The point is not that God is concerned about abstract mathematics but that he knows us infinitely well and cares about everything in our lives.

God is our real Father; in fact, Jesus says, "Do not call anyone on earth 'father,' for you have one Father, and he is in heaven" (Mt 23:9). God is the perfect parent whom we can trust without reserve. Our natural parents are just kids who grew up and had kids themselves and often failed to live out their best intentions for us, but we can forgive them and rejoice in the wonderful love of our Father God, who reserves the fullness of fatherhood to himself.

So many people I pray for see God as too busy, too preoccupied, too righteous or too distant to meet their deepest needs for love and intimacy. And I want to tear out my hair, rebuke them and shake them out of their false pride in thinking they are too small for his concern, out of the myopia that sees him as too small to manage the universe and them too. This grieves the Holy Spirit, who is trying to woo them into acceptance of the Father's intimacy. Jesus laid down his life for each one of us that we might know the depth of his desire for intimate relationship with us.

Norman grew up with a busy, disinterested father and was wounded by the lack of relationship with him. As we prayed, he remembered one occasion as a boy when he sat at the kitchen table to the right of his father and tried to tell him about his favorite comic-book hero, Spider Man. After a few moments, though, Norman's father lost interest and left.

I briefly explained the dynamic of contemporaneity to Norman and asked if he could see or sense that Jesus was there.

"Yes, he's on my right side."

"What is he doing?" I asked.

"Just sitting there."

"What are you doing?"

"I want to tell him about Spider Man."

"Why don't you?" I encouraged.

"Well, Jesus, Spider Man is this really cool guy who was bitten by a radioactive spider, and now he has magical powers and can spin webs and swing between buildings and cling to vertical walls, and . . ."

As Norman continued sharing with Jesus, his voice quickened and his emotions intensified. When there was a brief pause, I asked Norman what was happening.

"Jesus is saying, 'Wow, no kidding? Spider Man was something! Tell me more.' "

Jesus was meeting Norman at his point of deepest need and doing what his father had been unable to do. Jesus was saying to Norman, "I'm interested in you, I want to be with you, I want to talk about the things you're interested in. I like you, you are neat to be with, I love you."

Norman was then able to receive Jesus' love and begin to accept and love himself more fully. He was free to let go of bitterness toward his father and began discovering new ways to relate to him.

Love never fails. Love always finds a way. Peter says, "Above all, love each other deeply, because love covers over a multitude of sins" (1 Pet 4:8). The word translated "deeply"—or "fervently" in the KJV—can mean "stretched out." Stretched-out love, the love of Jesus that stretches out to embrace and enfold the other, is the kind of love that covers over many sins and their effects. This kind of love defeats the lies and schemes of the enemy, who tries to convince us that we are no good, worthless, not worthy of God's care and protection, doomed to loneliness and despair.

Over and over we have found that love gets the job done, for only love is tough enough, stretched out enough, resourceful enough, caring and intelligent and patient and capable enough to surmount every obstacle. Love never fails.

Sometimes at the end of a prayer session it seems that not much has happened. But later we discover that "love found a way." Our taking time to be with someone in prayer and conversation is itself a demonstration of God's love that begins the work of healing. Our motivation is not to be successful but to be faithful, loving and obedient, following the Holy Spirit's direction and walking with people in the path he provides.

Forgiveness

When someone sins against you and you do not forgive that person "from your heart," a seed of bitterness takes root in your heart and makes evil welcome to come and dwell there. Jesus warns in the parable of the unforgiving servant (Mt 18:23-35) that unforgiveness, if not dealt with, will have dramatic consequences. Unforgiveness has rightly been called the cancer of the soul, and it is perhaps the greatest block to emotional and spiritual healing. It gives room to bitterness, anger, hurt, rage and other tangled emotions that block our emotional and spiritual growth.

Unforgiveness creates an inner prison, and the only key to open the prison door is forgiveness. Our prayer should always be that God would override our pride, stubbornness and desire for revenge, and bring us quickly to forgive so that we may receive his abundant mercy and forgiveness ourselves (Mt 6:14).

Until we have pulled up any roots of bitterness or anger by forgiving, there will be insufficient deep emotional healing. But pulling up roots of bitterness is not easy. We often feel that we have the right to be angry and bitter because of the trauma to which someone's injustice has subjected us. We may have been physically or emotionally abused at a time when we were unable to defend ourselves. Still, God's rule is firm: we are to forgive others as we have been forgiven.

Through inner healing, the deep-level resentments, hatreds and angers that fuel our unforgiveness can be brought to the surface and seen for what they are—an ugly cancer bent on destroying us. It appears that harboring resentment can cause punishment to one's own body. The subconscious—which controls involuntary functions such as secretions, heartbeat and breathing—gets the notion that punishment is due someone because of the conscious mind's bitterness. And the subconscious, unaware that the anger is toward someone else, applies it toward what it controls: one's own body.

This explanation is surely too simplistic. Yet we have encountered scores of people whose arthritis began to be healed when they genuinely released others from their bitter judgments.

I (Doug) prayed for a young man named Carlos whose scoliosis in his middle back had moved his spine nearly three inches out of alignment. Upon interviewing him, we discovered that he harbored bitterness, anger and hatred toward his father and brother, who had both abused him. Carlos confessed and renounced his bitterness. Then he forgave his father and brother and turned them over to Jesus for mercy or judgment. In the next few minutes his back began to be healed.

Over the next hour, as we prayed in Jesus' name with faith and authority against the curvature, we saw a remarkable shift of nearly two inches in his spine and the shifting and realigning of muscles and tendons. One of the prayer team, a premed student, exclaimed, "Wow! Did you see that? No doctor could do that. Jesus really *is* the Great Physician!"

Sometimes we are afraid to forgive others because it seems to give them the power or permission to hurt us again. But actually the contrary is true. It is when we *do not* forgive that we continue to give people negative influence over our thoughts, our actions and, as explained above, even our bodies.

When I was finally able to forgive the person who had hurt me most, and to do so by asking him face to face to forgive me for hating him, I felt foolish; he was not able to understand or to ask my forgiveness or even to receive the forgiveness I offered. But afterward I came into total freedom from this person and the hurtful events he had caused. Because of his actions I had built a wall of anger and unforgiveness for self-protection, but the act of forgiveness broke the wall. I discovered that my protection was in Jesus, not in my bitterness, and that this person had no more negative influence in my life. I saw more clearly the destructive nature of anger and bitterness and am now eager to make forgiveness a way of life.

Reading Psalm 35:12-14 one day, Mike was convicted to pray and fast for a man he felt to be a sworn enemy. That day was one of the most painful and depressed he had ever spent. But just before going to sleep,

Mike suddenly realized that he had been carrying that man's burden all day long (Gal 6:2).

"Oh Lord," he groaned, "I didn't *know!* Oh God, have mercy on him! If that's what he has to deal with every day, he doesn't need an enemy in me." And from that day on, Mike has felt nothing but compassion for the man.

While it is difficult to forgive others, it is often even more difficult to forgive ourselves. Because of shame from sin or self-hatred arising from trauma or abuse, we find that we ourselves have become the enemy we need to forgive and to love (Mt 5:43-45).

Emily, whose story I told at the beginning of chapter four, was filled with shame and self-hatred because of past sin and abuse. Then the Holy Spirit showed her from Scripture that Jesus was praying for her and accepting her. Would Jesus forgive her for past sin? Yes! Could she then forgive herself? This, for Emily, was much more difficult. Through prayer for inner healing, Jesus helped Emily to see that her false pride and willful holding on to shame were causing her to hate what God had made good. She then asked God to forgive her, and to help her forgive herself.

Some of our strongest bitterness is directed toward God: *Certainly God could have prevented the abuse, hurt or trauma that has happened to me. Where was he, and how could a loving God allow such things to happen?* We have prayed with individuals who have survived satanic ritual abuse and other unspeakable traumas and hurts. We have wept tears of agony, questioning how God could allow these things to happen. But even in these worst circumstances we have learned to trust God and to encourage others to bend their wills in the direction of forgiveness, to work with God in overcoming evil with good. "Father, forgive them, for they do not know what they are doing" was one of Jesus' last utterances from his place of torture and death.

Satan, our enemy, is bent on destroying us. And while it often seems that he is winning the battle, God still keeps his hand on us and "works for good" (Rom 8:28) through even the worst disasters. The cross of

Christ is itself a pledge that God is most powerfully at work where all seems lost. Much of our suffering was caused by sin in ourselves and others, but we need to be ready to see that God *was* there and that Christ is ready to bear the pain and heal the wounds—even to use the devil's actions for redemptive purposes.

Jesus is saying, "I love you and have given my life for you. Forgive others, and you will be forgiven." The power of forgiveness—toward others, ourselves and God—opens the floodgates of heaven and brings the deep healing that we desire and that God intends for us.

Exchange

From the very first inner healing that I (Mike) took part in, exchange was at the heart of the experience. In chapter two I told how the Lord guided me to pray that a woman's hurt and rejection be exchanged with Jesus' healing and acceptance; and, in fact, the darkness in her heart was replaced with light.

Exchange is a central dynamic of the saving work of Christ. We see this clearly in 2 Corinthians 5:21: "God made him who had no sin to be sin for us, so that in him we might become the righteousness of God." The dimensions of this exchange are staggering. The sinless Jesus *became* the fact of sin itself so that sinful people could be divested of their sins and invested with the righteousness of God.

This exchange was accomplished at unimaginable cost to God. Think of the pain it caused him to take all the sins of humankind and identify his Son with them on the cross. When Jesus cried, "My God, my God, why have you forsaken me?" he was reeling from the righteous blast of the wrath of God at the sins of humankind, for Jesus was now identified as the fact and principle of sin itself. This was utter separation. This was final punishment. And Jesus accepted it so that "in him we might become the righteousness of God."

Inner healing is one of the ways we actualize his promise that we can experience and, in fact, be identified with "the righteousness of God." It requires the deliberate releasing into Jesus of our sins and of the sins against us, so that the exchange is complete, flowing in both directions.

By its nature, exchange is always a two-way transaction. In the market, the seller gives you the product and you give her the money. At your job, you give your employer your time and skills and he gives you a salary. Friends give each other care and understanding over the course of their friendship. The same is true of our relationship with God. We give him our faith and he gives us new life. We release hurt to him and he releases healing to us.

"He himself bore our sins in his body on the tree, so that we might die to sins and live for righteousness; by his wounds you have been healed" (1 Pet 2:24). Here Peter agrees with Paul's assessment of the dimensions of the exchange, adding the concept of healing to that of justification: the unwounded Jesus got wounded and our wounds get healed. This is precisely what the messianic predictions of Isaiah 53 asserted: "He was pierced for our transgressions, he was crushed for our iniquities; the punishment that brought us peace was upon him, and by his wounds we are healed" (v. 5). Isaiah 53:4 notes the nature of our illnesses: "Surely he took up our infirmities and carried our sorrows." Matthew's quote of that verse (Mt 8:17) uses the Greek words *astheneia* and *nosos* for "infirmities" and "sorrows." *Astheneia* means "lack of strength" and is used to designate the weaknesses the Spirit helps us with in Romans 8:26 as well as the curvature in the spine of the woman Jesus healed in Luke 13:12. *Nosos* is used at least a dozen times to refer to "disease." Such Scriptures make clear that Jesus' sacrifice for us extends not only to our sins but also to our emotional and physical maladies.

Underlying the dynamic of exchange is the assumption of covenant. Covenant says, "We agree to make an exchange. Your part is that and my part is this. You keep your part and I'll keep my part." Covenant usually includes certain signs. The sign of the covenant between persons and God in the Old Testament was circumcision. In the New Testament it's baptism. In business it's a contract. In marriage it's a marriage license and a rite. God has bound himself by his covenant to enter into a giving-and-receiving relationship with us. We give him our hurts, he gives us his healing; we give him our faith, he gives us answers.

The writer to the Hebrews indicates that God would be a liar and a perjurer if he did not make good on his covenant promises to us: "Because God wanted to make the unchanging nature of his purpose very clear to the heirs of what was promised, he confirmed it with an oath. God did this so that, by two unchangeable things in which it is impossible for God to lie, we who have fled to take hold of the hope offered to us may be greatly encouraged" (Heb 6:17-18).

In inner healing, Jesus and the person to be healed enter into an exchange. Jesus says, "Because of my love for you, I don't want the hurtful things of the past to determine the present condition of your self-image, feelings, attitudes or behaviors. So I will take those negative factors from you, but you must agree to release them to me. If you don't give them to me, I won't take them. But if you do release them, I will replace them with the good things of God. Just as you released to me your sin when you accepted me as your Savior, so you can also release to me your hurts, fears, shames, angers, lusts and lacks. In exchange for them I will give you my healing, assurance and forgiveness."

The exchange between Jesus and the wounded deals not only with what has been *done*—particular sins and attitudes—but also with who we *are*. Jesus takes away the false images we have of ourselves and gives us his own true estimate of who we are. In inner healing we learn to agree with his estimate of us and count it as the actual truth.

I once received an inner healing by meditating on Eph 1:6, "He hath made us accepted in the beloved" (KJV). As I reflected on that verse, I realized that Jesus is the Beloved. His own acceptability, which he earned through maintaining purity and obedience to the Father, is imparted to us as a gift. If we have accepted Jesus as Lord, then the Father imparts Jesus' earned acceptability to us—who have not earned it—and chooses to see us as acceptable as Jesus because he sees us *in* Jesus. If we then see ourselves in Jesus, we can lay hold of his acceptability and enjoy that inner harmony for ourselves.

The way this exchange takes place is usually straightforward. The prayer of exchange can be as simple as "Lord, I ask you to take away Rhonda's hurt and give her your healing." I find it helpful to remember as I say this that on the cross Jesus did indeed receive into himself the hurt we are praying about, and that it did indeed die when he died; that his resurrection from the dead permits him to replace the pain with his victory, and that he is doing so as we ask him.

Sarah had been born with a cleft palate and could not speak until she was almost seven years old. During the first eighteen months of her life she underwent multiple corrective surgeries, and occasional surgeries continued into her early years of school. Sarah told us that when she was a baby, her grandfather carried her out into the backyard and, holding her up to the sky, pleaded with God to "let this child speak!" It was not difficult for us to imagine the kind of pain, humiliation and embarrassment that Sarah endured as a child; yet she persevered through school and chose a vocation as a speech therapist!

As we asked God to shed light on her painful past, Sarah had a clear picture in her mind of being held by Jesus in the kitchen of her grand-parents' house. Jesus was slowly turning around until the baby's face came into view. Suddenly baby Sarah opened her mouth and screamed at the top of her lungs, and adult Sarah saw the cleft palate and remembered and felt all the horror and pain she had endured. Then, as the baby continued to scream, she saw Jesus put his finger into the baby's mouth until peace and contentment came upon her. She realized in a flash that Jesus had been there with her, had experienced all the pain and horror with her, and was now ready to take it completely upon himself.

A few minutes later, Sarah remembered a severe beating she had received from her father. She saw herself as a young child, crying, crouched in a corner, with dark bruises on her bottom and lower back. When we asked if Jesus was there, she said, "Yes. He is across the room with his back turned to me. He doesn't have a shirt on, and I can see his wounds and stripes. Now he is turning to me and saying, 'Sarah, I love you and have given my life for you.' "

From that moment, whenever Sarah remembers the painful events of her childhood, she sees a montage with Jesus in it, turning defeat into victory. The sting of the pain is gone. The exchange is complete.

*   *   *

There are a number of other dynamics that relate to the ministry of inner healing. As you read through this book, you will learn about the authority of Scripture, community, wholeness of personality, and guidance by the Holy Spirit. We may call upon any or all of these as we seek to bring Jesus Christ's healing love to the memories of his children.

Here we have highlighted the authority of Jesus, reframing, contemporaneity, love, forgiveness and exchange because they are *key* dynamics, without which one cannot expect to be effective in the ministry of inner healing. As various examples of inner healing are described throughout the rest of this book, ask yourself which dynamics are at work, and mark them in your mind. We are certain you will encounter these healing dynamics if you seek this ministry for yourself or for others.

In the next chapters, what we have been discussing so far will be made more practical as we explain processes for praying inner healing for oneself and others.

7
PRAYING FOR ONESELF

The *first six chapters of this book have provided definition, testi-*
mony, theological and scriptural foundations along with explanations of
the core dynamics of inner healing. At this point, as Paul did in his
letters, we shift from a theoretical to a practical outlook. You've already
picked up much about how to pray for inner healing from the illustra-
tions we've given. Now we want to spell it out more clearly.

One January back in the 1970s the Lord said to me, "Mike, this year
I'm not going to heal you physically through your own prayers." I tested
that and found that he meant it. This forced me to become more open
to and connected with others in the body of Christ. But I've always been
able to pray for myself for *emotional* healing, and the result has been
much inner peace and well-being. So in this chapter I'd like to show
why and how we can pray for inner healing for ourselves.

Why Pray for Oneself?

The first reason for praying for yourself is practical: you have more opportunity to seek your healing than others do. Your time, interest and energy are at your disposal, even when others are busy.

Another important reason for praying for your own inner healing is that some dimensions of healing are just not obtainable otherwise. God's use of you for your own inner healing is itself a healing that cannot come any other way. It's a bit like learning to tie your shoes. When you were four or five, tying your own shoes helped build a healthy self-respect that no amount of parental tying could accomplish.

When God heals you through your own prayers, you begin to take more seriously some of the wonderful things his Word says about you: that you're the friend of God, that you're a prince/princess, that you are operating in faith, that your old life was put to death in Jesus's death on the cross, and that your new self is being released into greater vitality through his resurrection. When you pray for yourself and it works, your hopes begin to rise, leaving the impossible in the dustbin and surging into the present excitement of the probable.

This is not pride; it is the healthy self-assessment of those who have found themselves "in Christ." Jesus, of course, was the most humble man who ever walked this earth. He was so humble that he emptied himself of all his divine attributes and prerogatives in order to become a man. He was humble unto death. But he also displayed a healthy self-assessment, for he had the boldness to call himself the very "Son of God," a "greater one than Jonah," a man who was "one with God." He accepted the worship of those who fell at his feet.

So we see that humility is not self-effacement; it is straightforward agreement with what Scripture says about us. It is not self-rejection; it is the grateful knowledge and acceptance of oneself in Christ. It is enjoying who God has made and redeemed and is sanctifying us to be.

Finally, self-administered inner healing helps us address our potentialities, developing the fullness of the personhood that God has in mind for us. Not only does it deal with the negative past, but it also opens the positive future. It sets us free to pursue our fullness. We're all interested in being who we are, and none of us is thoughtless about our name, which has a lot to do with declaring who we are. The nineteenth-century Scottish preacher George MacDonald commented on the white stone with the new name on it that Jesus promises to overcomers in Revelation 2:17. Notice the tone of promise and of health in these words:

> The true name is one which expresses the character, the nature, the *meaning* of the person who bears it. It is the man's own symbol— his soul's picture, in a word—the sign which belongs to him and to no one else. . . . It is only when the man has become his name that God gives him the stone with the name upon it, for then first can he understand what his name signifies. . . . Such a name cannot be given until the man *is* the name. . . . To tell the name is to seal the success—to say "In thee also I am well pleased."[1]

Self-administered inner healing is a wonderful, faithful moving toward the new name that will reveal ourselves to ourselves. It is a grand way to "put aside the deeds of darkness"—ours and others'—"and put on the armor of light" (Rom 13:12).

Understanding Yourself Biblically
One of the reasons for disciplined and consistent reading of the Bible is that we saturate ourselves with it. And Bible-saturated people learn to think biblically, evaluate biblically and respond biblically to the situations they encounter.

According to 1 John 3:20, "If our heart condemn us, God is greater than our heart, and knoweth all things" (KJV). All of us have experienced that condemnation that comes from our own hearts. So did St. John. When our hearts are biased against ourselves, we have a responsibility to take God's side against our own hearts and affirm that God knows nothing against us, as his Word plainly declares in Romans 8:1.[2] If we have saturated our minds with the Word of God, the Spirit has a vast reservoir of concepts and passages with which to meet the allegations of our hearts.

God's answer to self-condemnation is that you have been made accepted in the Beloved. If *God* accepts you, who are you to reject yourself, or to agree with anyone else's rejection of you?

In addition, a biblically saturated mind will not be misled into praying falsely for oneself—or anyone else. I know of people whose prayers for themselves are unsuccessful because they excuse themselves from honoring their parents since their parents hurt them. That sounds reasonable, doesn't it? But Scripture plainly requires that we honor our parents whether they behaved honorably or not. A biblically saturated mind will be full of passages about forgiveness, faith, obedience and power, all of which the Spirit can use to help us honor our parents, which is itself a key to well-being: "Honor your father and your mother, . . . that it may go well with you" (Deut 5:16). Biblically informed obedience pays off!

Embarking on Prayer
Memories that have bothered you but have not paralyzed you are great candidates for self-administered inner healing. I now offer a process that I have found effective in praying for my own healing regarding such memories.

1. Cover yourself with protection. Satan was the one who originally schemed for you to be emotionally injured. As you approach God for the healing of the past, reduce Satan's influence by praying a prayer of protection: "Lord, I take upon myself the whole armor of God and declare that you are constructing a barrier around me to protect me."

2. Ask the Holy Spirit to guide you. The Spirit of God knows everything about your need and is the obvious candidate to lead you through this process.

3. Remember the event in which you were hurt. This is like running a videotape of the event in your head. Remember what happened: who said what? did what? in what sequence?

Here is what I remembered vividly on one occasion of prayer: In my teenage excitement to build up my body, I figured out a way to hang a chinning bar from the ceiling of our covered patio. But when my dad came home from work, he saw me chinning myself. He put down his lunch pail and approached me in visible anger. I feared he was going to hit me as he scolded me for spoiling the attractiveness of the patio.

4. Feel the feelings. It's important that you allow yourself to feel the impact on your emotions of what was done and said. How did the event make you feel? Put names or descriptions on the feelings.

Regarding the chinning bar episode: I didn't mean to ruin the patio, I was just trying to build up my muscles. I felt picked on, misunderstood and judged for something I hadn't intended at all.

5. Speak to those who hurt you. It is cleansing to speak out loud, as though those who hurt you were present. Tell them how you feel and what they've done to you. But be sure to tell them at the end that you forgive them. Don't be misled into thinking that you have to *feel* forgiving toward them; it is enough to make a willfully sincere statement in which you release them from guilt.

For example, in my chinning bar experience: "Dad, I thought you would be proud of me for trying to strengthen my body. Instead you are angry, which makes me bewildered and caught off-guard. And when you almost hit me, I got really afraid. I've got an awful sickening feeling in my stomach. I don't want to feel this way with you. I want you to approve of me. Why have you frightened me?"

When I had fully expressed those feelings, I said, "Dad, I forgive you for scaring me, and I'm sorry I didn't ask you for permission to build the chinning bar."

6. Let Jesus into the event. Ask yourself: "Where is Jesus in this scene?" Look for him. He *was* there, you know ("surely I am with you always"— Mt 28:20), so look for him.

There are two styles of praying at this point. One is to pray in the first person: that is, I receive healing as I envision Jesus from inside myself. He comes and touches *me,* speaks to *me,* heals *me.* The second is praying in the third person: I see Jesus *and* myself from outside, from a third-person perspective. Jesus goes and touches that young boy that

I was and speaks to *him,* touches *him,* heals *him.* It seems that the first-person style works better for some and third-person for others.

Regarding the chinning bar: I saw Jesus standing by the fireplace in the patio. He keenly observed the exchange between my dad and me.

7. Observe what Jesus does. This is the point at which the presence of Jesus moves from being passive to being active. See what he does. Listen to how he speaks to you. Notice how he deals with those who hurt you. Don't let the enemy tell you that you are making all this up; trust that the Lord is with you and intends to heal you.

Concerning the chinning bar: Jesus came over and put his hand on my dad's shoulder, calming him. Then he put his arm around my shoulder and held me close to his side, like a friend. Then he reached into my heart and took away the fear, which looked like a lump of coal. After taking the fear into himself, he put a lump of light into my heart and said, "I'm healing you, Mike; I won't let this memory hurt you or your relationship with your dad anymore." Then he put his arm around my dad's shoulder, squeezed him and winked at him. "It's all right, Jim," he said.

8. Actively participate in what Jesus is doing. Remember the principle of exchange: let Jesus show you what he is taking away from you and what he is giving you in its place. Then say, for example, "Lord, I see you taking away this rejection and replacing it with your acceptance. I accept your acceptance of me. Thank you that this memory won't negatively affect me as it has in the past."

And in the chinning bar example: "Jesus, thank you for healing me." My eyes teared up. "And thank you for healing my dad, too. Thank you for taking away the negative picture of myself that episode gave me."

9. Exercise your faith to seal the deal. The business of having faith (as distinct from the gift of faith) is almost purely a matter of the will, and the primary function of the will is to make decisions. Therefore one can conclude a prayer for inner healing by saying, "Jesus, I decide that you have touched this memory and that it will no longer negatively affect me in self-image, feelings, attitudes or behavior as it did in the past.

Thank you, Lord!" This is the point at which *you* move from being a passive observer to an active participant.

The final thing I said regarding the chinning bar: "Lord, I set my will to believe that your healing will prevent this memory from causing me any further pain." And it hasn't.

Incidentally, the chinning bar stayed up for twenty years. I only had to paint it to match the rest of the roof.

If It Doesn't Seem to Work

There are times when praying for yourself doesn't seem to work. This is true of any kind of prayer, not just inner healing. So here is a checklist of glitches—possibilities to consider when prayer for yourself has seemed ineffective.

☐ *Inexperience.* All of us are clumsy when learning a new skill. We haven't yet gotten used to the procedure, the timing, the kinds of things the Lord does—but in all these areas we will greatly improve with more experience. So keep on keeping on with it.

☐ *Overreaching.* Some people immediately choose the worst thing that ever happened to them to pray for. It's much better to try your hand at lesser traumas before tackling the big ones.

☐ *Supertrauma.* Sometimes a memory is so painful that you can't get close enough to it to pray for it. The mere act of remembering these traumas creates such unbearable pain that you can only run from it. In this event, you need to seek help from someone else, for the other person hasn't experienced the trauma and can wade in and pray for it.

☐ *Conscious sin.* Psalm 66:18 states that if we consciously hold on to current sin and refuse to deal with it in repentance and forgiveness, the Lord will not listen to us. This does not mean that you must attain total sinlessness before you pray. It does mean that God has a way of putting his finger on sins he wants you to deal with now. To refuse to deal with them is to hinder his work in other areas.

☐ *Hindered faith.* Some past events may have hurt you badly enough to sap your faith to believe that they can be healed. Faith is primarily an act of the will, but it can be very hard to understand and exercise faith if you assume that faith is an act of the emotions. Here again it's wise to get help, allowing someone else to have faith on your behalf.

☐ *Misunderstanding faith.* If you can't *feel* that Jesus is healing you, and therefore believe that he isn't, you may be operating on a misunderstanding of faith. Faith, as I just noted, is more a matter of the will than the emotions or the intellect. We have feelings and thoughts about what we believe, of course, but the act of belief itself is primarily a matter of will.

If you believe that faith is emotional, and your emotions condemn you through the damage they've sustained, then you're in a quandary about how to believe. If you believe that faith is intellectual, and your thoughts condemn you on the basis of logical reflection on experience, then you're in another quandary about how to believe. But when you realize that faith is primarily willful, you are free to exercise your faith in agreement with Scripture even if your emotions or intellect have difficulty getting on board with the exercise of faith. This doesn't mean that God is anti-intellectual, but that faith often propels us into the realm of the *transrational,* that which is beyond the ability of the intellect to fully apprehend. The consistent experience of Christians is not "I believe because I understand" but "I understand because I believe."

Of course it's one thing to read about willful faith in a book and quite another to go out and put it to use in your own life. But that's what it comes down to, isn't it? Our advice is that you start saying something like this to the Lord: "Lord, I set my will—in cold blood, if necessary— that you forgive me when I ask for forgiveness," or "I decide that you're at work in me because I've asked you to, not because I do or don't feel you at work," or "I decide that you're actually doing what I thought I saw you doing in my prayer time."

☐ *When you can't see Jesus.* Our experience is that when someone can't see Jesus, it's because Jesus' authority to be there is blocked, or something else has greater authority to be present. (You might want to review the first half of chapter five, "Jesus' Healing Authority.") Worry, fear and pride are the kinds of blocks we've encountered. The solution is to ask, "Jesus, is there anything here that blocks your authority?" When something comes to mind, it will need to be repented of and/or renounced and replaced by allegiance to Jesus. Then the inner healing should proceed normally.

☐ *Onion-layered hurts.* A few painful events may have pierced you at several layers, like a nail stuck half an inch into an onion. These memories may need to be prayed for at successive levels. Our experience is that a considerable length of time may occur between dealing with different layers. Perhaps you will have to internalize or digest healing at one level before you're ready for it at a deeper level.

☐ *Unrealistic request.* It won't work to ask Jesus to prevent something in the past from happening. It did happen! You must believe that Jesus wouldn't have allowed anything to happen that he can't redeem and heal once it's brought to him in faith. So instead of asking him to *change* history, you can ask him to *heal* history. Again, the primary safeguard against this mistake is saturation with the Bible.

☐ *Not feeling healed.* One of the results of successful inner healing is that we feel different. Sometimes there is an immediate change in our emotions, but often it takes more time. When you don't yet feel the healing you've prayed for, you might say something like this to the Lord: "Well, Lord, I've prayed for this the best I can, and I'm now going to leave it on deposit with you. I decide that you're at work in this and that I'll feel it when you determine that I should. Show me what else to pray for if I've missed something. Meanwhile, give me the fruit of the Spirit, which is patience."

Healing Through Meditation on Scripture

The Word of God is "living and sharp," it "will not return . . . empty," it is "like a hammer that breaks a rock in pieces," and it "will never pass away."[3] There is enormous power in the Word to minister directly to our inner hurts and to stretch our deepest self toward that new name that God is eager to give us. I have found the following process of scriptural meditation helpful—and healing.[4]

1. Pray. Pray that the Lord will open you to his Word and open his Word to you. Pray to see Jesus in his Word.

2. Read. Read the passage through two or three times so that the sequence of events is clear in your mind. This process works best with scenes from the historical books—Old Testament events, the Gospels, Acts—because events are more easily digested than concepts. To illustrate the process let's use Luke 5:1-11, the miraculous catch of fish.

3. Picture.[5] Pretend you're a TV camera, and imagine what the scene must have looked like. See the events unfold as you would watch a film.

I think of Peter when Jesus told him to let his nets down. I see Peter in his boat, having listened to Jesus teaching from the stern of a boat. I hear him complain that he has been letting his nets down all night without result. I see that he agrees anyway. I see the amazement on his face as he realizes that the all-time fish story is in the making. I see him fall at Jesus' knees, imploring the Lord to go away from him. I see Jesus answer him.

4. Project. In this step, you project yourself into the roles of the persons in the story.

Be Peter as he doubtfully lets down the net at Jesus' direction. Imagine what it felt like to be him. I am the professional fisherman, after all; what does Jesus know about fishing? What do I feel when the great school of fish piles into my nets? Why do I tell Jesus to get away from me?

Then be Jesus as he checks in with the Father and gets the impression that he should tell Peter to let down the net. Tell Peter. Observe the result. See Peter fall to his knees and bid you get away from him. Feel what it might have felt like to smile, lift him to his feet and promise you'll make him a fisher of people. Think the thoughts Jesus might have thought.

Projecting is the heart of the process. It's at this stage that the Spirit especially speaks to your heart and mind. I never understood Pharisees until I had stood in their boots a number of times and felt their feelings and thought their thoughts about Jesus. Until then, I wasn't much worried about Pharisaism. But after *being* one in meditation, I had a clear understanding that Pharisaism was alive and well in the church today.

I never understood key factors in the viewpoint of God until I had put myself into Jesus' place. When I put myself in his shoes, I suddenly saw the validity of his curse of the fig tree. Being Jesus, I saw why the Pharisees were so dangerous to the kingdom of God. Seeing sinners through Jesus' eyes showed me the depths of his compassion for them. I acknowledged his priorities as I looked at his tasks through his eyes.

And I did not notice the almost unrelenting challenge Jesus presented to his disciples until I put myself in their heads and face to face with him.

☐ "*You* feed them," Jesus said to Philip about the five thousand and some hungry people who were milling around. And I gasped in disbelief, as I'm sure Philip did.

☐ "What were you talking about on the road?" he asked his band, who had just been bickering about which of them was the greatest. And I looked down in shame as they must have.

☐ "Come," he said to Peter on the edge of the boat. And I thought, "Are you nuts?"

☐ "Are you so dull? Do you still not understand?" he lambasted them. And I thought, "Gee, I didn't understand it either."

5. Resolve. The first four steps almost invariably teach you something that requires a resolution: to change an attitude, a priority, a behavior, a belief, an opinion, a procedure, a relationship or a feeling.

These five steps take about fifteen minutes to complete. If you want to gain the fullest benefit, take another fifteen minutes and write down what you've learned and resolved. I buy books with lined pages at the stationer's for this purpose. Over a dozen of them sit on my shelves as testimonials to one of the most valuable spiritual exercises I have discovered.

Over and over the Lord has used scriptural meditation for my emotional healing. Let me illustrate this with a couple of examples.

When I was a good bit younger and still having a running battle with temptations to use pornography, I meditated on the passage in John 8 regarding the woman taken in adultery. It was easy to project myself into her situation, for I had committed adultery in my heart scores of times. As I stood before Jesus there in the temple court, surrounded by my accusers, I knew that I was guilty and deserving of punishment.

But then the Pharisees crept away, and Jesus said, "Where are they? Has no one condemned you?"

"No one, sir," I answered.

"Then neither do I condemn you. Go now and leave your life of sin."

As I heard those words, the mercy of God did something miraculous, on two levels. First, it swept aside my very real guilt over having given myself to the use of pornography. This was a wonderful blessing. But even more important, it pierced through to hurts and unfulfilled yearnings that went all the way back to my childhood and that had fueled my desire for pornography. The sins were the weed, but the wounds were the root. From that moment on I had much less difficulty with temptation from pornography. Jesus' refusal to condemn me came to me as a promise more than a warning: "Go now, you are able to leave your life of sin. My mercy has healed you of what was urging you into sin."

I think Jesus could apply the Word to me so deeply because I had taken care to put myself in the woman's place. I had made myself pause and really internalize her situation. I had imagined what she was thinking and feeling; I had identified with her. Because I was identified with her sin and her need, I could also be identified with her forgiveness and healing.

Another example: When my first son, Kevin, was born, he was nearly seven weeks premature. His immaturity gave rise to a lung condition that caused him to turn blue and threatened his life. For several days he alternated between turning blue and recovering. Three days after his birth I spent most of one night in a church in prayer. I was twenty-one, I didn't know much about faith, and I was in agony. The next day he recovered and remained well—thank God! But I was left with a still-open wound, the agony I had experienced that night in prayer.

That wound stayed open until a couple of years ago, when I happened to prepare for a sermon by meditating on the sketch of the Canaanite woman in Matthew 15:21-28. You remember that her daughter was suffering terribly from demonization.

As I took the role of that woman, I found myself rebuffed *four times* by Jesus and his disciples! First he did not answer me a word. Next his disciples tried to get him to send me away. Then he disqualified me as a member of the group he ministered to. And fourth he made racial slurs about me.

Each rebuff had the effect of strengthening my determination to get healing for my daughter. And finally I heard him say, "You have great faith! Your request is granted."

That meditation put me through all the elements of my agony over Kevin's condition: anger, confusion, shock, self-doubt, despair, pain and teeth-gritting hope. Suddenly I saw that agony in a new light. It seemed to me that Jesus had put the Canaanite woman through the rebuffs in order to solidify her determination that her daughter be healed. Something about her faith was underdeveloped until Jesus challenged it to grow. And something about my young faith had needed the same challenge in order to release the Lord to do for Kevin what he wished to do: heal him.

It no longer hurts me to remember that near tragedy. The memory has been healed.

Paul wrote to the Romans that words written for Abraham "were written not for him alone, but also for us" (Rom 4:23-24). The words that Paul wrote, that Luke wrote, and that many others wrote were not simply for those who first received and read them but also for us. If we regularly open the Bible, the Holy Spirit will find portions of it to instruct, warn, bless, inspire, correct and heal us at any given moment in our walk with God.

8

PRAYING
FOR OTHERS

Lord, *how are you praying for Katy? What do you want to* happen today?" I (Doug) asked as we began praying with Katy. Quickly I saw a picture of Jesus, his knee bent to the ground, lifting a limp little girl up into his arms. He was preparing to give her mouth-to-mouth resuscitation, to raise her from emotional death to new life in him.

"Thank you, Holy Spirit," I whispered under my breath. "Now guide us and use us in bringing healing to Katy."

Katy Bauer was the second oldest and the first girl among six children of alcoholic parents. Growing up, Katy was the caretaker of the family. She was expected to be a perfect child and to do what she was told. Her dominant childhood memories were of a father who regularly threatened to put her up for adoption and who always gave preference to her brothers.

"My father stopped hitting me when I was thirteen," Katy told us, "not because I was becoming a woman, but because I wasn't worth anything.

My theory is that the worst always happens. If I don't expect too much, then I won't be disappointed."

Katy fought constantly to gain a place for herself in the family but was left struggling with depression, self-hatred and loneliness. She grew up feeling that love had to be earned, and that she had never received enough.

*   *   *

In the previous chapter Mike reviewed some of the practices and methods involved in praying inner healing for oneself. Inner healing often takes place during solitary times of prayer and the natural daily experiences of growth in intimacy with God and obedience to his Word and will. But often inner healing requires the loving support and care of friends or a trained prayer team who are open to the guidance of the Holy Spirit and ready to be used by God. This is especially true in the first experiences of inner healing, when there has been major trauma, or when one's faith is weak because of self-hatred or doubts about God's goodness.

I experienced the first steps of inner healing from the effects of my father's death before I knew anything about inner healing prayer. Then, as I prayed with a loving friend and we asked the Spirit to reveal the roots of my fears and anxiety, a breakthrough occurred in my under-standing and identity. This experience of being prayed for gave me insight and boldness to pray for myself and to be open to receive more prayer from others. Every experience of inner healing brings increased confidence and boldness to "ask, seek and knock" and to receive more of the Holy Spirit—more of the life and intimacy that God promises and desires for us (Lk 11:9-13).

Inner healing requires a deep openness to the Holy Spirit and will-ingness to be vulnerable to God and to others. One must be ready to share hurts, fears, shames, angers and lacks so that what has been fes-tering in inner darkness can be brought to light and exposed to the love and power of God. Praying for oneself, receiving prayer from others and praying for others are all part of the dynamic process of maturing in Christ described in Ephesians 4:13 and Colossians 1:28.

In this chapter, then, we will outline the "how to" of praying for others: knowing when to pray, what kind of preparation and awareness is helpful before praying, some methods and practices that have proved helpful during prayer times, and how to discern results or the seeming lack of results. Along the way we will continue to tell the story of Katy Bauer, using her experience of inner healing over several prayer sessions to illustrate the steps of inner healing prayer for others.

Background and Preparation

There are several factors that need to be in place within the person who seeks healing, and there are also a couple of steps to be taken by those who intend to pray.

1. God's timing. The initiative is with God. Our Lord's steadfast, never-ending love has a boundless desire to bring conversion, transformation and deep-level healing. No matter what has happened to us in the past, in the midst of the worst possible circumstances God prepares a way.

> Every valley shall be raised up,
>> every mountain and hill made low;
> the rough ground shall become level,
>> the rugged places a plane. . . .
> He tends his flock like a shepherd:
>> He gathers the lambs in his arms
> and carries them close to his heart;
>> he gently leads those that have young. (Is 40:4, 11)

> In all things God works for the good of those who love him, who have been called according to his purpose. (Rom 8:28)

> [Jesus said,] "You did not choose me, but I chose you and appointed you to go and bear fruit—fruit that will last." (Jn 15:16)

The brain records a memory of everything we have ever experienced, along with the accompanying feelings. Some of these memories can be recalled at any time, but others are buried deep in the subconscious. Some are so painful or traumatic that our conscious mind refuses to give them reality. We stick to denial so as to preserve desired thoughts about ourselves or parents or others who have affected us.

But in God's time these memories surface—in dreams, in quiet moments of reflection, through counseling or when an event triggers the memory of a parallel event. We begin to become aware of destructive patterns of fear, anxiety, anger or self-hatred. Finally we become determined to get at the root cause of such patterns. As we give ourselves to God and grow in trust and intimacy with Jesus, the Holy Spirit gently begins to press against the dark and hurtful things from our past and to bring them into the light to be healed. God is at work through all circumstances to bring healing and wholeness to us.

God was at work through the events of Katy's first two years of college to prepare the way for emotional healing. Away from home for the first time, Katy began to gain new perspective on past events. As she heard about the family backgrounds of others, she began to question whether things that happened to her were "normal" or right. But most important, Katy began to grow in her relationship to God. As a member of a strong Christian fellowship, she was involved in regular Scripture study and prayer. As she learned more about God's steadfast love and sacrifice to overcome our sin and brokenness, her trust and confidence in God's goodness began to grow.

God was reaching out to Katy through the circumstances of her life to draw her into a loving and healing relationship with himself. The Lord began to increase in Katy a desire to be healed and a willingness to trust in *him* for protection rather than in fear, anger or self-hatred.

2. Wanting to get well. If the initiative is with God, healing is possible only as we respond. It is impossible to bring healing to a person against his or her will. Healing requires openness to change and willingness to trust God and be vulnerable to the memories and events of the past.

We must be willing to face the past, to move past denial, to be honest and open, to fight patterns of fear or anger, to battle the oppression of the enemy—in brief, to *work* at getting well.

"Do you want to get well?" Jesus asks the man by the pool at Bethesda (Jn 5:6). The man responds with excuses, but there is desperation in his desire, and Jesus, seeing through this, commands him to walk. And the man responds.

If we too want to be well, then the truth—whether unconfessed sin, emotional damage, deep-seated shame or physical abuse—must be faced honestly. Patterns of anger, unforgiveness or denial, which were perhaps necessary for survival at an earlier stage of life, must be understood, faced and surrendered to God. There must be a willing desire to confront and work through whatever is there, even anger at God. We must be ready to wrestle with God in prayer. Inner healing prayer is a means God has given us of working with him to overcome sin and abuse. "If you hold to my teaching, you are really my disciples. Then you will know the truth, and the truth will set you free" (Jn 8:31-32). Inner healing requires an intentional, disciplined quest for truth.

Katy Bauer, learning to follow Jesus and surrounded by loving friends, dared to believe that good things *could* happen. She began to believe the promises of Scripture even over against her own hurtful past: "Fear not, for I have redeemed you; I have summoned you by name; you are mine" (Is 43:1). "Never will I leave you; never will I forsake you" (Heb 13:5). "There is now no condemnation for those who are in Christ Jesus" (Rom 8:1). Katy wanted to get well and was willing to wrestle with God, be vulnerable to the past and seek the truth.

3. Being willing to forgive others. Katy's wrestling with God began in earnest around issues of unforgiveness. In the midst of a conference on forgiveness during the spring term of her sophomore year, Katy suddenly came face to face with her anger, bitterness and unforgiveness toward her father. Scripture commanded forgiveness, but Katy did not want to forgive. She was *unwilling* to let go of her hatred and anger, because they had become part of her self-definition and of her protection from further hurt.

Yet Katy realized that her unforgiveness was blocking the flow of God's mercy to her. She wanted God to forgive her anger and bitterness and to help her to be willing to forgive her father.

Receiving healing requires facing the truth, giving the pain and anger to God, and being willing to forgive anyone who has hurt us. The person who has been victimized has good reason to be angry, bitter and un-forgiving, but Scripture teaches clearly that we must forgive others—as we have been forgiven by God—in order to *receive* the fullness of his mercy and forgiveness (Mt 6:14-15; 18:21-35; Col 3:13). Our forgiveness must extend to others, self and God.[1] On the cross Jesus paid the price for wrongs done to us, but we are responsible for our attitude toward these wrongs. An unforgiving attitude creates an emotional cancer that can destroy us.

Katy began the process of forgiving her father during that conference weekend. She asked God to forgive her for anger, bitterness and hatred toward him. And though she did not yet *feel* very forgiving, she deter-mined in her will to move in the direction of forgiveness and asked God to strengthen and support her. She took the extraordinary step of calling her father from the weekend retreat: she told him that she was a Chris-tian, recounted the things he had done to hurt her, and then said, "But I forgive you!" As Katy later commented, "He didn't take it too well."

Considerable pride and anger were still mixed with her forgiveness, but Katy was walking in the direction of God's mercy and healing.

4. Putting trust in Jesus as Lord and Savior. In her willingness to forgive, and in taking steps toward forgiveness, Katy was acknowledging the lordship of Christ and giving Jesus "faith permission" to exert his proper authority over the fear, anger, bitterness and hatred that had blocked the full exercise of Christ's authority and the flow of God's healing and forgiveness. In my experience, emotional and spiritual heal-ing comes as a result of an intimate relationship with God. As trust in God grows, the Holy Spirit gently begins to press against sin and darkness in our lives, opening a way for healing and forgiveness to flow.

During one period of my life, God awakened me every morning at 5:30 a.m. as if to say, "Doug, I love you, and I want to be with you today. Come and be with me, receive my heart and mind, hear and know my voice." From that time I have never doubted the reality of God's love for me. The experience of close intimacy with him gave me the strength, with his guidance, to examine and defeat the source of deep-seated fears and anxieties.[2]

5. Doing the homework. In preparation for a time of inner healing prayer, it is often helpful to reflect on past events and to journal or report any recurrent dreams, memories that carry powerful emotional overtones, or troubling patterns of behavior. It may also help to review the indicators that suggest a need for inner healing (see chapter one). We have regularly encouraged persons coming for prayer to take time to review their family history and reflect on the stages of their life, by age periods (womb to age five, six to eleven, twelve to seventeen, eighteen to twenty-one, twenty-two to thirty and so on), school years (preschool, elementary, junior high, high school, college) or another way of marking off time—years lived in one place, or significant events such as job losses and deaths in the family. It is important to ask what else was happening at the time of key memories—in the home, at school, with relatives. The key is to gather information to share in a more systematic way with the counselor or prayer team.

A person's willingness to enter into such systematic reflection is a powerful sign of his or her desire for healing, willingness to take responsibility for the past and motivation to move into a place where healing is possible.

6. Gathering and preparing a team. Often there is no choice but to pray one-on-one with someone. For long-term growth and healing, though, it is more helpful to gather a team of two or more committed people, including friends or partners of the one being prayed for. The presence of a prayer group multiplies wisdom, increases the ways by which God can lead through words of knowledge or wisdom, and brings confirmation of the direction God is leading. Following prayer sessions, it is very helpful to have supportive structures in place to provide continuing encouragement, prayer and accountability.

Katy's supportive friends and community were crucial for her healing. They provided love and encouragement, they witnessed God's love to her, and they encouraged her to receive counseling. Like the friends who brought the paralytic to the feet of Jesus (Mk 2:1-12), two friends brought her for her first session of inner healing prayer. It was natural for them to be a part of the prayer time, since they would provide the ongoing support framework for continuing healing.

7. Being open to the Holy Spirit's leading. Finally, in every phase of preparation for inner healing prayer, and in every stage of the healing process, it is necessary to remain open to the leading of the Spirit. God knew us before we were in the womb and knows every detail of our lives. He knows us infinitely better than we know ourselves and knows the exact progress and timing for the healing that we need. So those who pray and the one who is seeking healing are utterly dependent on the Holy Spirit's guidance. He is the source of healing.

The Prayer Session
We have found the following basic steps to be effective in praying inner healing for others.

1. Set the context. As you begin, review any pertinent information. Have the person summarize needs, problems or desired beginning points for prayer. If there has been no opportunity for preparation before the prayer session, briefly interview the person regarding angers, hurts, shame or any particularly painful experiences in the past; this will establish a beginning point for prayer. Give any needed instructions to the team or the person being prayed for. Then ask God to lead, reveal, guide, protect and bless the person during the prayer time. Command all evil spirits to leave and reject any of the enemy's schemes or devices to undermine God's purposes for the prayer time. Claim protection in Jesus' name.

2. Pray—listening to God. Ask the Holy Spirit to bring to mind any memories or events that need to be dealt with, and ask him to give the person courage, honesty and strength. Then wait on the Lord for what he is doing and saying. Take the posture of Jesus, who determined to do nothing except what he saw the Father doing (Jn 5:19). Ask Jesus to show you how he is praying for the person, since he is at the right hand of the Father interceding for us (Heb 7:25; 8:1). Seek to see or hear what Jesus is doing and saying, and be prepared to "follow after" him.

As we prayed for Katy, the Lord revealed that he wanted to breathe new life into her, to raise her from emotional death to emotional health. The image of Jesus on bended knee lifting Katy into his arms, preparing to give her mouth-to-mouth resuscitation, gave us a direction for prayer. Our task was to follow in obedience after Jesus, seeking ways to actively create what we had passively observed—to pray, under the guidance of the Spirit, for Katy to move from emotional death into life.

3. Ask questions. As you are praying and listening to God, be sure to ask questions of the person you are praying for as well as one another:

☐ What's happening?
☐ How are you feeling?
☐ Are you remembering anything?
☐ Is the Lord saying anything to you?
☐ Are you seeing anything?

Be alert especially to early memories or wounding experiences that may have opened a door for destructive patterns and emotions.

Often pictures of things that happened in the womb or during birth— revealed by the Holy Spirit—provide an excellent indication of fears, anxieties or betrayals that have oppressed the person because of parental sin or demonic influence in the generational line.[3] In praying for others, we have found that a mother's fear or anxiety, anger at a husband or feelings of being unloved, as well as the fact of an unwanted pregnancy or a failed abortion, may have an emotional impact on a child in the womb.

During our first prayer session with Katy, it became clear that her feelings of fear and of not being wanted went right back to her earliest childhood. When one of our group asked Katy if her parents had wanted her, she laughed bitterly, reminding us that her dad had often threatened to put her up for adoption. "Most of the time growing up, I wished that I hadn't been born at all," Katy said.

We asked Katy if she could let Jesus be with her in her earliest experiences in the womb. We began by laying a foundation of scriptural truth—that God had purposed her from the beginning, had knit her together in wonderful ways and had known her before she was in her mother's womb (Ps 139).[4] Further, Jesus had promised to be with her always, to the end of the age (Mt 28), and therefore had been present with her at every moment of her life and was present with her now.

We prayed through her conception and experiences as a fetus in the womb, reminding her that God knew her before she was conceived and that he had joined egg and sperm together, deciding her sex and her personality, and that he had *wanted* her. During this time of prayer, Katy had images suggesting that her father had often hit her mother while she was pregnant. Katy saw that there was fear and dread in the developing fetus, and that she had not wanted to be born. But Katy felt the presence of God—his love and his protection—even while she was in her mother's womb.

After a time Katy said she felt ready to come down the birth canal and be born. "See where Jesus is and what he is doing as you come out of your mother's womb," we encouraged her.

4. Invite Jesus to be present. For a memory to be healed, it needs to be remembered or reexperienced with Jesus present to remove the pain. Jesus is ready to be present as an observer—not to change the event, but to break its negative hold and take away the pain and fear. He will bring revelation regarding the experience or will reframe it, giving the person a new point of view. This is the key step in the process of inner healing, so let's take care to understand each part of it.

Jesus was there! You are not trying to imagine something that isn't true. Rather, you are allowing the truth to become apparent to one who did not have eyes of faith to see Jesus at the time of the event. Healing invariably comes when the person being prayed for is able to see or know intuitively that Jesus was there—to see what he was doing or saying—so he or she can accept Jesus' ministry and begin to understand events of the past in the light of Jesus' present care and love.

"Is Jesus there?" we asked, as Katy was reexperiencing being born in her imagination.

"I see him," Katy said. "He is one of the doctors. He has a sheepish grin, a warm smile, and he is waving his hand at me. There is incredible love in his eyes. He is saying my name, and he wants to hold me."

This image was confirmed by a member of the prayer team. We waited expectantly for a few moments, and then one of us asked Katy what was happening.

"He keeps asking if he can hold me, but I don't want to be held. I just want to be left alone!"

The person needs to be willing for Jesus to be present. For Jesus' presence to be effective, he must be welcomed and given authority over the situation. Is the person willing to trust Jesus and to invite his presence? willing to deal with anger, fear or anything that has usurped Jesus' authority? willing to let go of anything that blocks the flow of God's healing presence?

Be alert to false images of Jesus that may be present in the person's imagination due to demonic oppression. If the person sees or senses a presence that is in any way contradictory to our biblical understanding of Jesus—for example, a figure who frowns, who has an evil look or who hits or verbally abuses the person—then quickly state aloud that only the true Jesus is welcome and command that any false image or interference from the enemy be broken in the name of Jesus. The Holy Spirit is quick to expose the presence of these false authorities and to give guidance regarding anything that would hinder Jesus' authority in the situation. Work at this until all areas or issues where Jesus' authority has been compromised are understood and confessed. Breakthroughs come when one is willing to put everything under the authority of Jesus and to move in the direction of trusting his love and goodness.

Katy had been growing for two years in her love for God and her desire for him to be fully Lord. She was not yet entirely free of issues that posed threats to Jesus' authority, but none of these were strong enough to block her from seeing him present in her earliest birth experiences. The fact that Katy could see Jesus showed her willingness for him to be present and her willingness to give him authority and to trust him.

As Jesus was asking Katy if he could hold her, we encouraged her in prayer, reminding her of the scriptural truth of God's love for his children, that she was accepted and loved, and that there was no condemnation for her in Christ Jesus. Finally Katy said, "OK, OK, I'll let him hold me," and she asked Jesus to come and hold her. The moment she did so, Jesus took small Katy in his arms, lifted her up high above him and looked at her with the eyes of a loving parent. He blessed her with his grace and love to receive the truth in her inner being that she *was wanted.* Jesus spoke to her the same scriptural truths we had reminded her of—"I have made you, remember that. I have purposed you, and you are mine. I have made you and I love you. Do not argue with me about this."

As we continued in prayer for Katy, it seemed that Jesus wanted to hold her for a long time, to warm her up, to resuscitate her emotionally and spiritually through his own love. In prayer we encouraged Katy to stay in Jesus' arms and to hold on to him for "as long as it takes!" It seemed clear that the first picture I'd had of Jesus breathing new life into Katy was now being fulfilled.

After a while, though Jesus wasn't saying anything, Katy began to speak aloud to him, saying that she was hurt and angry, that she did not want to forgive her parents, that she was angry at herself and at him. "I'm no good, I'm not wanted and I was a big mistake!" she said.

To this Jesus responded: "No! I love you, I want you. I have made you in my image, and I will be with you. I know how you feel, and I

126   Inner Healing

know everything that has happened to you."

As Katy received Jesus' affirmation of love and acceptance, along with words of agreement and encouragement from the prayer team, she was finally able to agree that it was OK for her to have been born.

At this point it seemed as though Katy had indeed been "resuscitated." She was able to trust Jesus and to begin to agree with him against her past feelings.

Healing comes when a person can see or accept Jesus' presence in a painful event. A new view of God becomes apparent, along with a deeper relationship of love and trust toward God.

As Jesus was holding Katy, we asked if she could see what was happening to her parents, and we asked Jesus to show Katy what was happening. Katy saw her father walk into the room, take one look, see that she was a baby girl and walk out. He had wanted boys, and she was the second child and the first girl. Katy saw that her mother was distraught because of her husband's response and the brokenness of their relationship. In her grief and sorrow, Katy's mother was not able to respond to and receive her new daughter.

Jesus continued to hold on to Katy and warm her through his own love until she was willing to be laid in her mother's arms, though she held on to Jesus' thumb the whole time for security. During this time, guided through prayer, Katy was able to receive Jesus' compassion for her mother and take steps toward forgiving her. She also heard Jesus say some things to her father—even though her father could not hear them—and these words helped Katy to release some of her anger and hatred.

Jesus will usually touch, hug, speak words of love and encouragement, and provide a safe place. He will take away the exaggerated pain that Satan had used to cripple the person, leaving behind only the healed remembrance of a hurtful situation.

After Jesus had held Katy for a long time, warming her with his love, it seemed that he wanted to put her down and take her for a walk. We checked to see if she was ready, and she said yes. Jesus quickly took

Katy to a time when she was a little girl, about four or five years of age. She said she was in a deep, dark, cavernous place, and the two of them were climbing up a ladder to a trap door. A member of the prayer team received exactly the same picture, of Katy and Jesus coming up the ladder out of the trap door into a sunlit green meadow.

But Katy wasn't sure she wanted to come out of the cavern. Jesus continued to be with her and to encourage her; some of this encouragement came from the prayer team through words of knowledge and other promptings of the Spirit. Katy began to acknowledge that she did want to give up her sense of unworthiness, self-hatred and self-destruction. And then she was able to go through the trap door with Jesus and walk into the meadow.

Looking back, she said, "It's still dark back there."

Jesus responded, "I know. Do you want to do anything about it?"

Katy saw herself running back, closing the trap door and stomping up and down on it, saying, "I don't want you anymore. I don't want you anymore!"

Katy was shutting the door on her old "friends"—fear, rejection, self-hatred and abuse. Then Katy and Jesus romped in the meadow for a long time until she was tired and Jesus held her in his arms again.

In our postprayer session (see step seven, below), Katy admitted that she had put up with fear and rejection all her life, thinking they were part of her and she deserved her pain. But now, with Jesus' love and authority so real and tangible, she could begin to resist and work against these things that had bound and crippled her for so long.

Take time for Jesus to be present to other painful memories until the roots of bitterness, anger and shame have been removed. Once a person has experienced the presence of Jesus and knows his love personally, it is easier to invite him into other memories that need healing.

During this and other times of prayer for inner healing with Katy, the Lord Jesus took Katy to particular memories and experiences of her childhood and teenage years. Each time he revealed himself to her as one able to meet her deepest needs as friend, father, mother and lover.

One healed memory was of a time when Katy was in the seventh grade and lived in North Dakota in a one-room house with no running water. In Katy's own words: "As a family we would drive to the high school, fifteen miles away, to take showers and to do laundry. I hated these weekly trips. I was terrified of anyone seeing us at the high school, of finding out that we lived the way we did. While we waited for laundry, my four brothers, my dad and I went to the gym to shoot baskets.

"In my memory, I saw my dad standing at the free-throw line, challenging us kids to beat him. He and my brothers competed fiercely to make the most free throws. Even though I was second oldest, I still was ignored because I was a girl. I kept trying to make my dad watch me shoot, but he was too busy showing off for my brothers. I remember vowing that even though I missed now, I would learn to play this game, I would make him notice me, I would be a man—better than a man; I would be a basketball star and excel in sports.

"And then Jesus was there, teaching me how to shoot, putting the ball in my hands correctly, holding my arm, helping me push the ball. I kept missing; over and over the ball would clang off the side of the rim, but Jesus was not angry or impatient or frustrated. He even went to collect the ball after every miss. He laughed at my attempts, because they were completely unimportant to him. He just wanted to be with me. Finally, I made a basket. Jesus reached down and picked me up around the waist and held me high over his head, like a trophy.

"When he put me down and we stood laughing together, I noticed my dad standing and staring at us. I grabbed hold of Jesus' hand. He wanted to lead me out of the gym and away from my father. My dad asked what I thought I was doing, and I replied that I wanted to go with Jesus. The gym had two doors, one on each side. Jesus pulled me by the hand toward one of the doors. I wanted to go, I wanted to follow this man who was teaching me to play, but I kept looking back over my shoulder at my father standing alone on the free-throw line. I wondered what was going to happen to him, who would take care of him.

"As Jesus and I reached the door, I couldn't move. I just stood in the doorway, frozen in fear. I really wanted to step through the door with him, but I felt guilty about leaving Dad. I asked Jesus if it was really OK, if it was all right. (Yes, said the people praying with me.) My dad just looked at me accusingly, standing alone in the middle of the gym. Then he turned and walked out the other door, away from us.

"I was still standing in the doorway, scared and guilty. Jesus reached down, picked me up, lifted me over the doorstep and told me that he loved me and would take care of me."

5. Minister God's love. Your goal in praying inner healing for people is to be instruments of God's love and healing purpose. The best techniques in praying healing are nothing without love. The goal is to love the person being prayed for and to be faithful in following Jesus as he leads in acts of healing. Actively participating in what Jesus is doing— replacing love for hate, declaring acceptance where there has been rejection, encouraging forgiveness to defeat the power of unforgiveness, identifying and rebuking the false authorities that block Jesus' full lord-ship—is our exercise of love and faith in response to guidance from the Holy Spirit.

Love never fails. Time and again Mike and I have closed prayer sessions thinking that not much has happened and discouraged by our own ineptitude and inability to see or know what to do—only to discover later that taking the time to be with the person in prayer was itself a demonstration of God's love that began a work of healing. We are constantly reminded that our goal is not to be successful but to be faithful to our Lord's leading. He is the one who knows what needs to happen and the timing for each person's healing. He loves people far better than we ever can, and our privilege is to be instruments of his loving purpose.

6. Bless the person. Close and seal the prayer time by blessing the person. Let the Spirit be your guide in bringing to mind what he has revealed and done during the prayer time. For example, bless the person with continuing openness to the work of God. Ask God to fill every cleansed place with his light and love. Pray for strength and power of will to resist any challenge from the enemy at the places that have been healed. Pray for discernment and wisdom.

7. *Postprayer counsel.* Review what has happened; summarize what has been learned. Share anything the Spirit revealed during the prayer session that still needs to be verbalized.

Review any Scripture that came to mind during the session. You might suggest a pattern for regular study of Scripture. Remind the person that God's Word is a sword of the Spirit for protection and battle against the enemy. For example, remind him or her that God's love casts out all fear.

Avoid unnecessary counsel or lengthy advice. This is a time to encourage the person to walk in ways that will maintain and increase the healing God has brought. Encourage him or her in the spiritual disciplines of prayer, listening to God, worship and praise.

Finally, encourage the person to deal with these and other issues by receiving counseling and/or by meeting again to pray together.

Cautions

Many of the hindrances to prayer that Mike outlined in chapter seven apply also to inner healing prayer for others. As you pray for others, beware of the following tendencies in yourself.

☐ Try not to interrupt people's expression of feelings. Until you have honored their feelings by listening, you haven't won the right to give advice.

☐ Avoid being judgmental, condemning or laying blame.

☐ Let go of defensiveness if not much seems to be happening. Remember, you are called to be loving and faithful, not successful.

☐ Let God kill your curiosity. Be sensitive and caring, not intrusive or prying.

☐ Don't sermonize—"You've got this problem . . ." This hinders the truth and compromises your authority to minister Christ's healing. Try to say only what you see, hear or are commanded from the Lord.

☐ Avoid too quickly countering what the person is feeling. For example, if conscience is condemning him or her, listen until the feelings are fully expressed and then gently point out the scriptural truth that there is "no condemnation for those who are in Christ Jesus."

☐ Do not rely on one method. There is no one strategy or technique for every situation. Too heavy reliance on a particular technique or emphasis can turn into an attempt to manipulate or make something happen in order to produce an experience. Remain open to what God is doing. Every individual is unique, so look for the fresh word or revelation from God for that person. Remember, God knows that person completely; let the Lord bring ministry through you.

☐ Do not be afraid of failing. You must be willing to risk, to feel that things are out of your control, to respond faithfully to what God is doing and trust God with the results.

☐ Always take the lead from Jesus. *He* is the leader, not your imagination or past experience. Be cautious in imposing your imagination or even your words of knowledge on another unless there is confirmation. Move cautiously when acting on what you are observing. Wait for confirmation. Let Jesus bring to the person's mind what is to happen or what needs to be done. Do take risks of faith to follow what you are seeing and the guidance you are receiving, but proceed with caution. In receiving a word of knowledge, ask the Lord whether and when you are to share it. This serves as a check on your impulsiveness.

☐ Beware of going too long. It is easy to get caught up in three- to four-hour prayer sessions. It is OK to take a break, to come back and finish later, or to continue a day or a week later. Remember that healing is a process, and you are better off to limit and consolidate the work that is being done than to labor too long.

☐ After the prayer session, do not tell others about the person's problems unless he or she has given permission. Confidentiality is essential.

9

PSYCHOLOGICAL
FACTORS

In *many Christian settings, faith and psychology coexist in an uncom-*
fortable truce. Sometimes pastors encounter issues that are beyond their
expertise and feel forced to refer deeply troubled parishioners to psychologists. When they talk about it, you may catch a whiff of guilt: "I
should have been able to help him through prayer." But there are
psychologists who have felt precisely the same way when they are con-
fronted by obviously demonized patients and must refer them to the
church.

One psychologist was somewhat miffed at me (Mike) for having
cured his patient in thirty minutes when he had been working with him
for six months. And I reluctantly released a man with multiple personalities into the care of a psychologist who was much more equipped
than I to minister to him.

We should say at the outset that some of the difficulty is pride. Pastors are proud of their theologies, psychologists are proud of their psychologies. "What we have works!" both assert, and not without evidence. But pride knows no limitations of theology or psychology and "goes before destruction" (Prov 16:18) as effectively for psychologists as for pastors. Scripture does not declare that doctrine or theory never fails, only that love never fails.

Let's go deeper: often our pride is invested not so much in our academic disciplines as in ourselves. If I am a pastor and my pastoring fails to help someone, my ego is at stake, not just the theology I represent. And if I have a Ph.D. and find that all my knowledge fails to help a patient, my ego may be more tender than my theoretical constructs.

You are probably ready to point out that there is an all-important difference between psychologists who believe and those who don't. And I would agree. If one's spirit is dead through unbelief, then its rebirth is the first order of business. One day in my office I interviewed a troubled young married couple whose only problem proved to be that they didn't know Jesus. As soon as I introduced them to him, they went their way and didn't need any more counsel from me, for the basis of their trouble had been spiritual. But it is important to ask oneself the question of timing: is this the moment when this person has been prepared by the Spirit of God to say "Jesus is Lord"?

But there are those whose trouble has an emotional, physical or relational basis. Many of them can be successfully ministered to through inner healing, deliverance, physical healing and godly counsel. I fully expect that as these ministries widen and mature, we'll find that the needs of most troubled persons can be effectively met in the church. Nonetheless, so many people have been beaten up by the world, the flesh and the devil that there will always be a need for extrapastoral care.

It might help at this point to ask, What is psychology? Earle Fox, an Episcopal priest who practices inner healing in Pennsylvania, says, "Psychology is not a pagan disease, as some have implied. It is simply the study of human nature. Everyone has a 'psychology,' that is, a view of human nature." Fox points out that the phrase "in the image of God" in Genesis 1 ties theology, the study of God's nature, with psychology, the study of human nature. "It also means," he continues, "that if you want to understand psychology, you must know God. The personhood of God is the blueprint for the personhood of human beings."[1]

I am convinced that there need be no conflict between Christian psychology and pastoral ministry. A brief review of priorities can clear up much unnecessary competition: Are you a pastor who is a Christian, or are you a Christian who is a pastor? Which comes first for you? Are you a psychologist who is a Christian, or are you a Christian who is a psychologist? If one's relationship with Jesus comes before one's profession, one can appropriate truth from many quarters.

Useful Psychological Concepts
In 1975 I had the extreme good fortune to meet a deeply committed Christian psychiatrist. Over the years she taught me several psychological dynamics that have been invaluable in praying inner healing for others. I am well aware that my explanations of these dynamics are not as sophisticated as a professional might prefer, but they have served me well.

Omnipotency. This is a largely unconscious assumption that begins very early in infancy that the child has caused or deserved everything that happens to him or her. When the child is raised by healthy parents and circumstances are mostly positive, omnipotency serves to create a strong self-image. The self-centered childish mind assumes "I have caused these good things" or "I deserve these good things." This provides a solid basis for developing a healthy postadolescent concept of the self. But when bad things happen, the impact on the self-image is negative: "There must be something awfully wrong with me for this to have happened."

The sense of omnipotency tapers off through childhood, finally ending in adolescence. But its effects can continue until they are brought to the foot of the cross, where healing and redemption can be found. Many persons walking around in adult bodies are arrested at preadolescent stages of emotional development because of this dynamic.

A knowledge of this dynamic is of great value in inner healing, because most emotional damage occurs before one emerges from adolescence. It takes only a moment's reflection to realize that Jesus can be invited into early memories and can counteract the negative influence of omnipotency. "You did *not* cause your parents to divorce," he can say to a guilt-ridden omnipotent seven-year-old, bringing release from long-held and little-understood fears. Doug's ministry to Katy, whose self-hatred was an omnipotent internalizing of her father's rejection, included a healing in which Jesus specifically countered that rejection (see chapter eight). In so doing, he began to heal Katy of the negative effects of her sense of omnipotency.

When believing parents have sinned against their children, omnipotency can produce a confusing miasma of fearful impressions about God. The children get a double message: they hear "God loves you," but their omnipotency interprets the parents' sins as evidence that he should not or cannot love them. God is identified with the sin of the parent, and the child identifies himself or herself as the proper recipient of the negative treatment.

Projection. Projection also operates mostly unconsciously until one trains oneself to recognize it. Behind each of my current actions there is an intention: I intend to do something, and then I do it. Let's look at how this simple fact explains many of the problems we experience in our communications with each other, with the help of table 2.

☐ First, I only see my intention. I know what I *intend* to do, say or mean, but I am not aware of how I'm coming across to you. That is, I don't see my behavior. Who of us can be looking in a mirror all the time?

☐ Second, you see my behavior, but you do not see my intention. You see what I'm doing, but you don't know what intention lies behind my actions.

☐ Third, there is often a gap between what I intend and what I actually do. This is especially true when there is an emotional component in the transaction. For example, have you ever decided to be reconciled with

someone, only to have your attempts make matters worse? The exis-
tence of the gap tends to sabotage initial attempts at effective commu-
nication, because we *think* we're expressing ourselves accurately.

☐ Fourth, we unconsciously project our own intentions onto someone
else's behavior. Unconsciously, we look at someone else's actions and
ask, "What would *I* intend if I were doing that?" The result is represented
by the dotted line on table 2.

Table 2. The Dynamics of Projection[2]

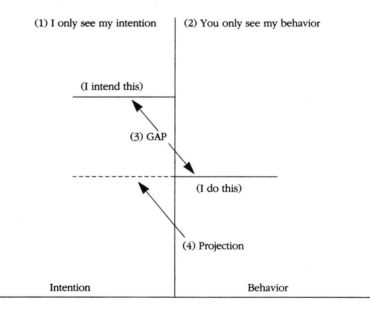

(1) I only see my intention	(2) You only see my behavior
(I intend this)	
(3) GAP	
	(I do this)
	(4) Projection
Intention	Behavior

These four factors are responsible for a vast amount of misunderstanding between people. When I have projected my own intention
onto your behavior and reacted to you, I am really dealing with *my
projection* instead of the real you. In emotional hurts, we frequently
project onto the person who hurt us the intention to hurt because that
is what we would have intended if we had acted as they did. What's
more, we hold on to these conclusions with remarkable tenacity. It is

obvious to us that the other intended to hurt us. It is so obvious that there is no need to confirm the conclusion. Right? Wrong!

If the process I have outlined in table 2 is accurate, then only *I* can clarify what I intended; and only *you* can tell what effect my behavior had on you. You have to say things like this: "I was deeply hurt by what you did. Did you intend to hurt me?" And I have to say, "My intention was to do thus and so."

If you discover that I did not intend to hurt you, your inner healing occurs almost automatically. Many persons continue for decades to carry wounds that were never intended by the supposed wounders.

In chapter five, in the section about reframing, I recalled how one day I felt I needed inner healing for a rejection from my wife, who had ignored a bid for intimacy. I kept on saying to myself, "I forgive her," but I still smarted from the rejection. Finally I decided to tell her how I was feeling and express my forgiveness. After I explained, she responded with amazement, "I wasn't rejecting you, I thought you were joking." Her explanation of her intention served to wash away my pain immediately.

Individuation. Regarding marriage, God's Word says, "A man will leave his father and mother and be united to his wife, and they will become one flesh" (Gen 2:24). Today this separation from parents is usually called "becoming one's own person" or "individuation."

Preparation for taking leave of one's parents actually begins at about two, continues through childhood and picks up a great head of steam in adolescence. The defiant-sounding "No!" of the two-year-old is not rebellion but the beginning of the assertion of selfhood. The parent who whacks a two-year-old across the face in response to such a "No!" is not correcting rebellion but quenching selfhood. The child is not intending to rebel—he or she doesn't even know what rebellion is. A two-year-old "No!" is an expression that "I am!" Since the child is made in the image of I AM, what more appropriate declaration?

A frequent reason inner healing is needed is that parents projected an adult-level meaning on their child's "No!" and assumed that the child's intention was rebellion when actually it was a joyous declaration of "I!" Think of the shock of declaring "I!" to other "I's," only to have them beat you for it.

Individuation is often a turbulent process. Part of its difficulty is that nothing stays the same for the child or the parent. Just when you've settled into mutual understanding, something changes and it feels as though you're back to square one.

Clearly, the child's degree of authority and freedom has to be renegotiated frequently. When the child is twenty-one years old, he or she should have had a lifetime of experiencing increasing levels of authority and freedom over his or her own life.

I remember a day when my first son, Kevin, suddenly piped up from the back seat, "Can I walk home from here?" I laughed spontaneously at the absurdity of the request: he was ten years old, and we were on the freeway, miles from home. To have let him walk home from there would have been criminally irresponsible.

But as I thought about it, I liked his bid for more authority and freedom. So about half a mile from home, I pulled over to the curb and put him out, saying, "See you at home, son." He was ecstatic.

"Don't worry," I said in response to his mother's worried look, "he'll be OK." And when he arrived home, there was a new look of self-respect in his eyes.

What parents pretty consistently fail to notice is that *they* are the ones who must grant the growing authority and freedom their children need in order to mature. You have to give it to them. That is, it stops being yours and becomes theirs. Perhaps table 3 will illuminate this gradual, but constant, turning over of authority and freedom from the parents to the child. Parents can err by giving either *too much* authority and freedom (dotted line) or *too little* for the stage of development their child has attained (dashed line).

Both mistakes usually draw out what looks like rebellion from the child. Too much authority and freedom tend to move the child to "act out" in order to force the parents to restore their own authority and thus

Table 3. The Individuation Continuum

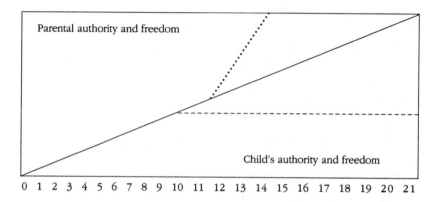

provide the child with security and boundaries. How many young people do you know who would say, "Dad, I'm feeling that I've got just a little too much freedom in my life, so I'd like you to clamp down on me"? They can't articulate the need, so instead they will abuse their privileges with the often-unconscious intent to get the parent to clamp down. On the other hand, the child with too little authority and freedom rebels for a different reason: the desire to break out of constrictions that are no longer appropriate.

Frequently, of course, this dynamic erupts in adolescence. The child is now getting more and more determined to "be my own self." And the only platform to kick off from is parents. Now it's time to *individuate.*

Paul wrote some great advice to the Colossians: "Children, obey your parents in everything, for this pleases the Lord" (Col 3:20). Some of what children need to obey is the command to exercise appropriate authority and freedom over their own lives. "Fathers, do not embitter your children, or they will become discouraged" (Col 3:21). Few things embitter children as much as too much or too little authority and freedom over their own lives.

Oppressive restrictions are an inappropriate response to the adolescent's God-given need for preparation to leave home. And to cop out and say, "I'm tired of fighting with you; do whatever you want!" is also to miss the mark. Very few parents are wise enough to mark out a perfect authority line between them and their children. So the parents project inappropriately on their children—usually assuming "rebellion"—and the children project inappropriately on their parents, usually with the notion of "control."

Inner healing is often needed where parents have responded poorly to the child's need for more or less authority and freedom. Parents sometimes need inner healing from what they perceive as rejection from their adolescents. Adolescents often need inner healing from controlling, fearful and anxious parental behavior.

Doug and I have seen problems surrounding individuation so often that we recommend that a prayer counselor always take at least a few minutes to check out the possibility of hurt in this area.

Numerous other contributions from psychological theory and research can aid in the ministry of inner healing, but a working knowledge of projection, omnipotency and individuation will go a long way toward making one useful to the Father of lights, who wishes to heal the bruised souls of children.

Faith-Psychology Conflicts

There are several problem areas to be discussed in the interaction of Christianity and psychology.

Worldview clash. One's worldview works as a filter to focus on what is possible or probable and what is not. One's values are often reflected in the worldview one espouses.

One example of worldview conflict between Christianity and psychology surrounds the question of sin. Many believing psychologists have been trained in secular institutions that teach deficient ideas about sin— or none at all. And, of course, nonbelieving professors know little or nothing about God's provision for sin in the sacrifice and resurrection of Jesus. I find that even Christian psychologists tend to gloss over the importance of confession and forgiveness. They often do not understand how much their patients need to see their sin and bring it to the cross.

Meanwhile, pastors tend to overlook the dysfunctional dynamics of a person's past as issues that need to be unearthed and addressed if lasting improvement is to occur.

Both pastors and psychologists should realize that since they have invested several years and thousands of dollars in their education, they are predisposed to ignore or even deny the contribution of another worldview. Where there is a flat contradiction between Scripture and psychology, Scripture must be preferred, of course. But let's be asking God if there is a scriptural base to the psychologist's viewpoint, and let's stay open to receive further light on all issues.

Exclusivity. When pastors refuse to allow their parishioners to visit psychologists, and when psychologists discourage their patients from seeking healing prayer, there is an unnecessary exclusivity going on.

Counselor is the only scriptural title shared by all three Persons of the Godhead. Psalm 73:24 refers to the Father as counselor; in Isaiah 9:6 Jesus is prophesied to be a counselor; and in John 14 Jesus refers to the Holy Spirit as "another Counselor." The word in Greek is *paraklētos—para*, to the side, and *kaleō*, to call. A comforter or counselor is one who is called alongside. Knowing this, we can conclude that we have a friend in the person of God. Another biblical counseling word is *noutheteō*, which means to put in mind. A third word is *boulē*, from the root meaning "will." These words suggest to me that befriending people, looking for truth to place in their minds, and attempting to influence their wills in agreement with the truth are important components of the counseling enterprise. You can do these things from both a pastoral and a psychological orientation.

Inner healing does not cancel the need for psychological counseling. Neither does psychiatry/psychology void the need for inner healing. I know of a number of very successful working relationships in which the psychologist's skill in bringing underlying issues to the surface is followed up with inner healing by a prayer counselor. Then the patient returns to the psychologist for more unearthing, which produces more material for the inner healer.[3] This relationship—which is expressive of the unity of the body detailed in 1 Corinthians 12—must indeed please the Father of lights, from whom all good gifts come (Jas 1:17).

Belief and unbelief. Sometimes a Christian needs psychological assistance but there is no believing psychologist in the community. Suppose the Christian visits a non-Christian psychologist and is asked to take the Minnesota Multiphasic Personality Inventory (MMPI), a common diagnostic test. If the Christian marks on the test her belief in angels, demons or healing, she may find herself evaluated as abnormal.

This is a matter of worldview clash. Unbelieving psychology is certain that those who believe in angels are delusional—and indeed they may be, quite apart from the objective reality of angels. But healthy people can agree with Scripture and for that reason alone be judged schizophrenic. This is hardly helpful.

When a patient must work with an unbelieving psychologist, my suggestion is that the patient and the psychologist straightforwardly agree to disagree about contested matters and focus on what they can agree on. Despite the disagreements, a Christian *can* benefit from a therapeutic relationship with an unbelieving professional. And in two cases I know of, professionals have been witnessed to so successfully by their patients that they are "not far from the kingdom of God." Mature prayer counselors, too, can work in concert with an unbelieving psychologist for the benefit of the patient without compromising their beliefs or the help available to the patient.

Insensitivity. Those who practice a ministry of inner healing without heeding what psychology teaches about empathy can become spiritual bulldozers. A friend who practices inner healing says, "I do not find it good procedure to quickly tell a person that they need to forgive. Rather, I want to use empathy skills to listen to the person in such a way that they feel deeply listened to. With significant hurt this will certainly take up virtually all of the first session; with deeper hurt it may take several sessions. Only when they can trust me and believe that I understand will I gently move toward issues of forgiveness. I say this because I know of many victims of sexual abuse and/or rape who were told in the first session by some well-meaning inner healer that they needed to forgive the person who abused them. The counselor had not earned the right to say such things, and the result was a compounding of the hurt rather than a healing. Empathy is a form of love, and love heals. Just listening correctly will bring healing."

Transference issues. Psychologists are well aware of this dynamic, by which their patients transfer (project) feelings toward their parents or others onto the professional. But few pastors or practitioners of inner healing seem aware of this dynamic, and many are puzzled by ungratefulness or even overt hostility from those they're trying to help. They can completely misread what's going on, assuming that the negative feelings of the person they're trying to help are actually *aimed* at them instead of *being transferred* to them because they're trustworthy and safe. Pastors and inner healers who are confused by such responses would find that a good talk with a practicing psychologist would bring much wisdom.

Underdiagnosis. Because they're not psychologically trained, some pastors and inner healers blunder by underestimating the severity of their parishioners' emotional conditions. They may be miles out of their league and not know it.

Nevertheless, don't worry too much about damaging someone through ignorance. Jesus said emphatically, "Love one another!" If your intention has been to love people well, you won't hurt them much, even if you're ignorant of their real needs. If God has indeed called you to a ministry of inner healing, however, do seek to establish a close working relationship with an effective professional. Then you'll avoid serious underdiagnosis. When you chat with that professional, ask him or her about psychotic episodes, decompensation, and the medical etiology of symptoms.

Quite a number of inner healers have found that frustrated psychologists are referring clients to *them*. The temptation is to respond by throwing up your hands in defeat, exclaiming, "What can *I* do?" But don't be too hasty in declining those referrals. After you read chapters eleven and twelve, you just may find yourself in the thrilling position of helping a leprous Naaman. You can react to the referring psychologist as the king did: "Am I God? Can I kill and bring back to life? Why does this fellow send someone to me to be cured of his leprosy? See how he is trying to pick a quarrel with me!" Or you can react to him as Elisha did: "Why have you torn your robes? Have the man come to me and he will know that there is a prophet in Israel" (2 Kings 5:7-8). We have seen our God do marvelous things through simple, believing prayer.

Counseling Skills

Besides gaining familiarity with the psychological dynamics we've discussed—omnipotency, projection and individuation—we recommend that those involved in inner healing gain some proficiency in counseling skills. One need not earn an advanced degree in order to become a more effective *listener*. Putting yourself in the place of the person you are trying to help is one of the most effective ways to listen. Asking clarifying questions is a helpful skill: "Tell me what it felt like when your father said that to you." If you can identify with the person you are listening to, you have gained an important skill. A psychologist friend says, "The basics of effective listening are empathy, warmth and unconditional regard."

Reframing, which we discussed earlier in this book, is a helpful intervention (counseling technique). Another is *mirroring,* in which the counselor states back to the counselee what he is saying, but with a different enough slant to help the counselee gain a new perspective. This, of course, is very close to the *exposure of projection,* which is an exceedingly useful intervention. You might say, for example, "How do you *know* what your husband intended in that behavior?"

Self-disclosure by the counselor can be a very encouraging intervention. It allows the counselee to realize that other functioning people have struggled with issues and found healing through the grace of God. *Sharing of observation* is another helpful skill: "Do you realize that every time you mention your mother you clench your teeth?" You can learn to *field questions* in a way that helps the counselee. "Well, what do *you* think?" may be a good way to respond to a question.

The various disciplines and schools of psychology provide skills that can be used effectively. Client-centered therapy, for example, teaches many proven and safe procedures which the nonprofessional can profitably practice.

Again, ask a practicing professional for help and insight. You will learn to recognize when a situation is out of your depth and it is time to make referrals.

When to Refer
If you're an ordained pastor, you should already have a list of psychologists to whom you can make referrals with confidence. If you are a prayer counselor, when you are thinking of referring someone to a psychologist it would be best to consult with the pastor under whom you're ministering.

Here are a few rules of thumb:

☐ If someone we've prayed with three or four times shows no significant signs of healing, we will ask ourselves if a referral is needed.

☐ If there seem to be self-destructive or suicidal tendencies, we will recommend that the counselee, or persons responsible for him or her, seek the advice of a professional pastor or psychologist.

☐ Evidence of child or elder abuse, of course, requires that reporting laws be known and followed.

☐ Evidence of grave disability requires immediate professional assistance from those legally qualified to commit persons to mental institutions.

☐ If the person is already under the care of a psychologist, we will do nothing to jeopardize that professional relationship.

Legal Considerations

Ours is a litigious country, with more laws and lawsuits than the rest of the nations of the world combined. More than one church has been sued in its attempt to minister to individuals. There's not a lot of precedent to follow, but consider these suggestions:

☐ Consult with an attorney who is familiar with issues surrounding counseling and church ministry (such an attorney's services may be available through your denomination). In particular, ask about consent forms (see following), laws regarding notifying authorities when you learn of physical or sexual abuse, and malpractice insurance.

☐ If your ministry is conducted under the auspices of a church, ask the person you will pray for to sign a consent form something like this:

CONSENT FOR LAY MINISTRY

_____ Church
_____ (City)

I desire to receive ministry from the Prayer Ministry Team of _____
_____ [church, city and state].
I understand that the Prayer Ministry Team members from whom I am receiving ministry make no claim to be professional counselors in this prayer ministry, and I release them from any liability and do not hold them responsible for any present or future mental, emotional or physical condition.

I understand it is not the purpose of the Prayer Ministry Team to fulfill the role of mental health professionals or physicians, and if I am feeling homicidal, suicidal or dangerous to myself or others, I accept that the Prayer Ministry Team recommends that I seek professional help.

The Prayer Ministry Team agrees to meet with me once a week for three weeks, at which time we will together reevaluate the need to continue or terminate the relationship, based on the results of ministry.

All sessions are confidential except in group supervision where cases are discussed and recommendations made by the director of this ministry or the pastor of _____ Church.

   I have read, understood, and agree to all the above.

Signed:

_____   _____
(person requesting ministry)   (date)

_____   _____
(Prayer Team member)   (date)

_____   _____
(Prayer Team member)   (date)

☐ Make sure that your ministry is overseen by an ordained pastor.
☐ Recruit intercessors who will agree to pray regularly for protection from the world, the flesh and the devil.

10

FREQUENT MISTAKES

George Bernard Shaw's interesting slant on an old expression is thought-provoking: "Anything worth doing is worth doing wrong." At my (Mike's) church we state it a bit differently: "At St. Jude's, we value growth over success."

Both slogans are germane to a performance-oriented society like ours. Shaw is pointing out the need for trial and error, for nobody starts out as an expert. Valuing growth over success sets members free to experiment with new ministries. If all you have to do is grow, if you don't have to succeed, then you're free to try anything you might feel the Lord is drawing you to. After all, the Greek word for disciple—*mathētes*—means "learner," not "achiever."

This chapter is not intended as a witch-hunt to smoke out misguided inner healers. Many people who have felt drawn into this ministry have made mistakes. We have too. What I'd like to do here is share some of the mistakes we've run across, not so that you might pass some litmus test of errorless inner healing but so that you can profit from the experience of those who have gone before you. We want you to have a head start on effective ministry. For clarity, we have labeled the common mistakes under four headings: errors of understanding, of inexperience, of technique and of character.

Errors of Understanding

These mistakes are all related to the way we think about God, people and the healing process.

Deception. I am deceived when I am wrong but think I am right. Deception can come to us through our own thinking, the influence of others or demonic influence. Deception is deceptive. That may seem obvious, but it is amazing how many people will accept an eloquently expressed idea because it appeals to something in them, even though they know it involves a departure from Scripture.

Together, the Bible and the Holy Spirit are the great checks against deception. Scripture alone is not a sufficient check, for one can read the Bible with a wooden literalism or a cavalier liberalism, neither of which requires the least aid from the Holy Spirit. Either can improperly interpret the Word. The Spirit alone is an insufficient check, not because he can make an error but because we can "hear" him wrongly. We have all heard horror stories of actions based on the tragically simplistic rationale "The Lord told me to . . ." But together, the Spirit and the Scriptures provide solid guidance. It took the Holy Spirit to *write* Scripture, and it takes the Holy Spirit to *read* Scripture. As St. Paul observed, "All Scripture is God-breathed and is useful for teaching, rebuking, correcting and training in righteousness, so that the man of God may be thoroughly equipped for every good work" (2 Tim 3:16). But this same St. Paul also claimed, "The man without the Spirit does not accept the things that come from the Spirit of God, for they are foolishness to him, and he cannot understand them, because they are spiritually discerned" (1 Cor 2:14). The Holy Spirit enlightens Scripture, and Scripture authenticates the Holy Spirit's promptings.

In any ministry—inner healing or other—if a person feels guided in contradiction to Spirit-enlightened Scripture, he or she is in danger. How do you avoid that danger? How do you judge the inner impressions you receive during ministry? You need to ask yourself several questions:

☐ What has the church historically taught about this?

☐ Does what I think I'm hearing contradict the expressly written word?

☐ Does it contradict any of the great scriptural values, such as faith, hope, love, truth, righteousness?

☐ Is my heart peaceful about the matter?

Preferring psychology to Scripture. Psychological theories and methodologies should never occupy the same level of authority as Scripture. When we allow the conclusions of the latest psychological study to compromise the veracity and integrity of Scripture, we have misunderstood the highway markers of reality.

When a "recent study" challenges Scripture, try this: wait six months. Undoubtedly another study will challenge the questionable one. Keep sticking to Scripture, keep asking for more light on it, keep trusting the Holy Spirit to guide you into all truth.

Immature demands for total, immediate healing. When some people discover the ministry of inner healing, they lose any sense of perspective and timing. Assuming that ministry, relationships, education and occupation must stay "on hold" until they're all fixed up, they pull back from all these important elements of life. These people misunderstand that life is a process. You get healed *as you go.*

This is an important concern, for we have seen committed, gifted, available people pull out of valuable service to the church and the world because they've discovered they have wounds that need to be addressed. "I'll resume ministry once I'm well" seems to be the sentiment. They may even develop supporting theology: "Health begets health; therefore I can't be used for others until I'm well myself." If promoting the kingdom of God is important, a charismatic Narcissus is as immobilized as a hedonistic secular one.

Encourage those you pray for to go on with life—education, career, relationships, ministry and recreation. It is easier to guide a moving ship than one that is anchored in the harbor. God wants you to be healed. Healing will come as you go forward. Inner healing works best on site, not on the shelf.

Errors of Inexperience

Under this category we put mistakes that we and others have made simply because we lacked experience to know differently.

Immature expectations of your own health. The most usual manifestation of this mistake is to assume that you must be all healed before you can be used to heal others. I have had the rather interesting experience of being used for the healing of a condition in someone else *before* that same condition was healed in me. Had I believed I had to be healed first, very likely neither the other person nor I would have been healed, for the Father used my faith for the other's healing to increase my faith to lay hold of my own healing.

Not facing yourself. This may sound like the opposite of the mistake I just described. On several occasions the Lord has brought three or four people with the same problem into my office, one after another. This is always the cue that there is something in *me* that he wants to address. Here is a truism to memorize: *We accept others in direct proportion to how much we accept ourselves.* If I find myself hostile to people, it is because they touch off something in me that I haven't yet dealt with. So when the third wife-beater, alcoholic, thief or philanderer in a row crosses your trail, you might ask God: Is there something in me that you want me to look at?

Idolizing inner healing. Inner healing is not the greatest thing since sliced bread. Jesus Christ is the greatest thing since—and before—sliced bread. Inner healing is like a pair of pliers: you want them in your tool kit, but they're not appropriate for every task. Inner healing does free up the operation of some other gifts, such as physical healing and deliverance from demonization, but it is not the center of the ministerial world.

Unresponsiveness to the Spirit. Sometimes the Spirit will give you a clear impression of what you're to do as you minister to someone. One of our young team members kept hearing the words "twenty-five years" while ministering to someone at a recent conference. The idea of twenty-five years didn't make sense, so the team member ignored it and talked about issues that seemed more relevant. But the person's healing didn't occur until the team member finally asked about "twenty-five years." It turned out that the person's condition had begun twenty-five years ago, and once that was known, it was apparent how to heal it. We must be willing to appear a bit foolish if we are to collaborate effectively with the Holy Spirit.

Errors of Technique

Here we address certain misuses of inner healing methods.

Misuse of imagination. In chapter one we promised that we would deal with this concern thoroughly. Our understanding is that those who are opposed to utilizing the imagination use some or all of the following arguments:

☐ New Age groups encourage people to use their imaginations in non-biblical or antibiblical ways.

☐ Almost all occurrences of the word *imagination* in the Bible are negative.

☐ Christians should carefully avoid occult practices—see, for example, Deuteronomy 18:9-13.

☐ Therefore Christians should not visualize or use their imaginations in the service of God.

I am no expert in occult or New Age practices, but I have no doubt that occult healers utilize their imaginations in opposition to the will and word of God. I would expect them to. Why?

First, because Satan is a usurper. Not satisfied to be the loveliest among the angels, Satan set his sights on usurping the place of God himself. Satan wants to exercise dominion in every place where God intends to rule: the heavenlies, the earth, governments, social structures and the human heart. Second, Satan is a compulsive imitator of God. He counterfeits the genuine articles of God. Does God use prophecy? Then Satan counterfeits prophecy in divination, astrology and the like. Does God use angels? Then Satan deploys his demons to usurp the place of God and his hosts. Does God use the printed word? Then Satan inspires writers to produce books, even to call some of them "holy."

It is dangerous for the people of God to use the counterfeits Satan has created. Why not, if they work? In fact, they work because they're plugged into Satan and he has power. Those who use Satanic mechanisms will find themselves harmed, sooner or later. Most persons who are demonized have come into that state because they have disobeyed God's Word and engaged in forbidden behaviors.

But is the human imagination a creation of Satan? I can think of no one who would believe that. Imagination is not a satanic counterfeit of a godly capability. Rather, imagination is a godly capability that can be misused. The usurper is at work to pollute the godly gifts the Creator has given us.

Can you misuse your tongue? Of course. Does that mean you stop using your tongue altogether? Of course not.

Can you misuse your eye? Yes. Does that mean you should stop using it? No.

Can you misuse your *inner* eye? Yes . . .

What is the definition of *misuse?* It is using some thing or some capability under the inspiration of Satan rather than of God.

The capability in question is the imagination, the ability to visualize. There is no question that one can visualize in opposition to the will of God. But it is foolishness to allow the usurper to preempt a gift God has given us because it is possible to misuse it.

Part of the problem is linguistic. There are seven Hebrew and four Greek words that are translated "imagine" or "imagination." The KJV translates so thirty-three times. But the NIV only manages to get those eleven words into "imagine" or "imagination" eight times. Those same Hebrew and Greek words are also translated "meditate," "purpose" and "think." Surely the fact that we can think wrongly does not mean we are not to give up thinking!

Jesus used his imagination. Over and over, the Gospel of John records his saying that he did only what he saw his Father doing, that he spoke only what the Father gave him to say. In the same Gospel he says the Father is a Spirit. If the Father is Spirit, and Jesus did only what he saw the Father doing, how did Jesus see the Father? Certainly not with his natural eyes.

When Jesus spoke forgiveness to the man let down through the roof, the teachers of the law said to themselves, "This fellow is blaspheming!" Most translations say next, "*Knowing* their thoughts, Jesus said . . ." (Mt 9:4). The Greek word for "knowing" here is actually *idōn,* which means "seeing."[1] I think Jesus saw their thoughts in his imagination. How did he "know" them? To what in him did the Spirit direct that information? Those who are experienced in receiving words of knowledge from the Holy Spirit realize that they often "know by seeing." And so I will continue to defend the spiritual use of the imagination. Where we make mistakes, though, is in using imagination without guidance—imagining what our own mind produces, visualizing what has not been given by the Spirit of God. At best this practice is useless; at worst it is occult. It is, therefore, crucial that we verify the source of our impressions. Be sure to study the section on discernment in chapter eleven.

Here is the crux of the issue: Does the Holy Spirit still speak "trans-biblically" to the followers of Jesus Christ today? Does your theology allow the Holy Spirit to say, "Turn left at the next corner," even though that phrase cannot be found in the canon of Scripture?

Asking someone other than Jesus to be the healer. No one but Jesus Christ took our sins and illnesses upon himself on the cross. No one but him has the authority or ability to heal in the power of God. So it is misleading to ask God to use someone else to accomplish healing. Once I overheard someone say in a prayer for inner healing, "Now let's just have your father apologize for beating you." That's a no go. It will take Jesus to do the healing. This leads to the next mistake.

Trying to change history instead of heal it. History happened—period. It's no good pretending that something didn't occur. Earlier in this book we mentioned the error of praying for God to change history instead of heal it: "If only the event hadn't happened! Aha! Let's ask Jesus to go back in time *before* the event and keep it from happening." This is misguided sympathy, a kind of deceptive thinking that ends up misleading both the prayer minister and the one receiving ministry. Both know, at some level, that it is a lie, but hope that God will use it anyway.

The thing *did* happen! It is pretense and foolishness to hope that it didn't.

What we need is an enlargement of understanding. Supposing that since God is in charge of time, he can go back before an event occurred and prevent it betrays a faulty concept of God's almighty power. God doesn't have to prevent history, for there is nothing that the world, the flesh or the devil can think up or accomplish that is beyond God's power to redeem. It is enough to ask God to heal the effects of history.

Overusing one method. Just when you discover a prayer style that works—such as one of those we've outlined in this book—you encounter someone who cannot respond to that style. Do you force them to use your style? No, you go looking for Jesus to show you a way to which they can respond.

Errors of Character
The following errors can afflict both the one who ministers inner healing and the one who needs to receive it.

Lack of humility. Pride is always a major mistake. It is, after all, Satan's sin: trying to insinuate himself into the rightful place of God. If God could deliver a sophisticated message through a donkey, he doesn't *need* you to heal someone. He is so kind as to *choose* to use you. "What do you have that you did not receive?" Paul queried. "And if you did receive it, why do you boast as though you did not?" (1 Cor 4:7). Do you have a technique which God uses to heal the sick? Where did you get it? Do you have a desire to heal the sick? Where did you get that desire? *Everything* in us that is of use to others has been received.

Abuse of trust. When God anoints us for ministry, it draws people to us. We must guard against abusing the favor we have in their eyes. The newspapers tell story after story of pastors who have abused their authority and seduced those who came to them trustingly. You might think you'd never do anything as ugly as that, but be warned: they didn't start out planning to seduce anyone either.

There are lesser abuses of trust also, such as allowing those who receive your ministry to aggrandize you. Don't let their misunderstanding of your anointing elevate you in their minds.

Impatience. Most people didn't get damaged in a flick of time; they probably won't get healed in a flick either. In some cases it would be catastrophic for healing to occur instantly. People need time to move into the new dimensions of personality, viewpoint and emotion that inner healing brings. The Father is doing his work at the pace he knows is best. Be patient. Besides, your patience is healing to those who've often been hurt by the impatient.

Savioritis. This is akin to pride and the misuse of trust. It is when the prayer minister or the one who receives prayer thinks that the minister is something wonderful. That God works through people is to the credit of God rather than the people he works through.

Alternately, savioritis is the assumption that God cannot accomplish his wonders without you. There is only one Savior.

Refusing ministry for yourself. Peter's response to the footwashing in the upper room illustrates two frequent mistakes. When Peter exclaimed, "You shall never wash my feet," Jesus answered with a stunning rebuttal and threat: "Unless I wash you, you have no part with me" (Jn 13:8). Some people assume that Jesus was referring to the cleansing accomplished by his blood, but Jesus' comment two verses later reveals a different intention: "A person who has had a bath needs only to wash his feet." The issue here is not salvation but discipling. Jesus is saying, "Peter, unless you *accept* ministry, you'll never be qualified to *give* ministry."

Early in your discipling, you must experience what it feels like to receive ministry; this is a crucial part of learning sensitivity to those to whom you'll give ministry.

Demanding excessive ministry. Peter's other mistake was to demand, "Not just my feet but my hands and my head as well!" (Jn 13:9). The character issues here are mistrust, impatience and self-centeredness. It is counterproductive to demand that those who know how to do inner healing drop everything and everyone else and attend to you until you're satisfied. Likewise, it is counterproductive to let people make such demands if you know how to minister inner healing for others. The healer and the one seeking healing both need to be looking to Jesus for help *and for the pace of the help.* Jesus knew what Peter needed and was insistent about giving him no more and no less. He still knows what's best for you and those you minister to. Pandering to self-centeredness will not help us to outgrow it.

Demanding full understanding. There are times when you just don't know much about what's going on between Jesus and the person you're praying for. I've had the frustrating experience of praying for people who were quite miraculously healed but were nearly inarticulate when I asked, "What happened?" They simply couldn't put it into words. Finally the Lord told me to give up trying to comprehend *what* had happened and just gave thanks *that* it had happened.

* * *

While these mistakes of understanding, inexperience, technique and character are important, the greatest mistake is not to risk following God's leading because you are not yet a fully mature expert. No ministry springs full-grown and mature—thank God! In his gentle kindness and caring compassion, the Lord lets us grow bit by bit so that we have time to digest what we learn and become his disciples over the long haul.

11

WORKING
WITH THE
SPIRIT

After *the 1990 Urbana missions convention, where we led the* ministry team, I received the following letter from a man named Tom:

Dear Mike,

I just wanted to take a minute to tell you how grateful I am for your ministry during the recent conference in Urbana, Illinois. I went to take a group of college students from our church and really had no expectation of God doing anything for me. How wrong I was. For the past two years I have been going through a period of depression and anxiety that I couldn't seem to shake off. There was no particular reason for any of it that I could see. I had been praying and fasting for some time concerning this. The Lord kept reassuring me to trust him but didn't give any direction as to what to do. During your ministry the Lord really touched me. He exposed the roots of problems that went back to events in my childhood and then set me free from them. Since then I've had no more problems with depression and anxiety. You can imagine what a joy it is to be free from all of this.

I am also very appreciative of the other counselors who were there. Their sensitivity to the Holy Spirit was in much evidence as they prayed for me. I remember two times when they prayed for things that were tremendously significant for me that they *could only have known through the Holy Spirit* [italics mine].

Our God is committed to working through people. He could, of course, do everything necessary for everybody everywhere in the next two minutes, all by himself. But since he is an incarnationalist up to his hairline, his deliberate choice is to limit himself to working through us. This, of course, necessitates our learning how to collaborate effectively with him.

The team members who prayed for Tom managed to listen to the Holy Spirit, who knew exactly what lay at the root of Tom's depression and anxiety. In this chapter we'd like to share with you what we taught our team members when we were preparing them for that ministry.

Fellowship with the Spirit

Jesus' last will and testament, if we might use that phrase, is found in the first paragraphs of Acts. Jesus was about to return to the Father, and here he gives final instructions to his disciples. While eating with them, he said, "Do not leave Jerusalem, but wait for the gift my Father promised, which you have heard me speak about. For John baptized with water, but in a few days you will be baptized with the Holy Spirit" (Acts 1:4-5).

The disciples seemed to be interested in eschatological matters, but Jesus directed them back to what *he* considered crucial: "It is not for you to know the times or dates the Father has set by his own authority. But you will receive power when the Holy Spirit comes on you; and you will be my witnesses in Jerusalem, and in all Judea and Samaria, and to the ends of the earth" (v. 7). Those are Jesus' last recorded words before his ascension back into heaven.

Notice that what the disciples had seen and heard of Jesus up to this point was not yet enough to equip them for effective ministry. They had been in his company for three years. They had seen all the healings and miracles. They had heard all the teachings. They had even gone out on limited missions and had *themselves* preached with power, healed the sick and cast out demons (Mt 10; Lk 9). They had watched Jesus die and they had touched his risen body. Why were they yet unready for their ministries? What did they still lack?

What they lacked is indicated in Jesus' prediction, "You will receive power when the Holy Spirit comes on you" (Acts 1:8). Hadn't they had power when they went out on mission? Yes, they had, but apparently it was of a limited nature and duration; now it was to be replaced by a more extensive and permanent empowerment. The disciples' pre-Pentecost experience seems similar to that of Old Testament figures on whom the Spirit came for certain purposes, only to leave them after those purposes were fulfilled.[1]

This is in no way to state that the disciples didn't already have the Holy Spirit *in* them. Every believer has the Holy Spirit within. Nearly forty days before, on Easter night, Jesus had already given them the Spirit: "And with that he breathed on them and said, 'Receive the Holy Spirit. If you forgive anyone his sins, they are forgiven; if you do not forgive them, they are not forgiven' " (Jn 20:22-23). Probably this impartation had particular reference to the authority to forgive sins, received when they inhaled Jesus' breath, as it were.

Nonetheless, Jesus seems to have thought that in some sense the Spirit was not yet *on* them, or was not yet in them in *fullness.* The word *baptized* may give us a clue. Acts 1:5 says, "For John baptized with water, but in a few days you will be baptized with the Holy Spirit." The sense of the word *baptized* is immersion or saturation. In baptism the subject is covered with something—with water for repentance, and now with the Spirit for empowerment.

It won't do to get very dogmatic about how the empowering of the Spirit occurs. In the book of Acts there are at least five different ways or sequences in which it happens. On the day of Pentecost the Spirit came upon the 120 without human mediation, and "all of them were filled with the Holy Spirit and began to speak in other tongues as the Spirit enabled them" (Acts 2:4). Two chapters later, after an account of a prayer meeting, the identical language is used: "And they were all filled with the Holy Spirit and spoke the word of God boldly" (4:31). Hadn't they been filled on the day of Pentecost? Yes. So why did they need to be filled again?

In Philip's ministry in Samaria it is clear that there was a brief time between salvation and empowerment. Acts 8:12 clearly states, "But when they believed Philip as he preached the good news of the king-dom of God and the name of Jesus Christ, they were baptized, both men and women." This is salvation! Now look at verse 14: "When the apostles in Jerusalem heard that Samaria had accepted the word of God, they sent Peter and John to them. When they arrived, they prayed for them that they might receive the Holy Spirit, *because the Holy Spirit had not yet come upon any of them;* they had simply been baptized into the name of the Lord Jesus. Then Peter and John placed their hands on them and they received the Holy Spirit." This is empowerment!

Paul also seems to have experienced a two-stage initiation, being fully converted on the road to Damascus (Acts 9:5) and then receiving the Holy Spirit three days later at the hands of Ananias (9:17).

But in the house of Cornelius, the order was reversed:

While Peter was still speaking these words, the Holy Spirit came on all who heard the message. The circumcised believers who had come with Peter were astonished that the gift of the Holy Spirit had been poured out even on the Gentiles. For they heard them speaking in tongues and praising God. Then Peter said, "Can anyone keep these people from being baptized with water? They have received the Holy Spirit just as we have." So he ordered that they be baptized in the name of Jesus Christ. (Acts 10:44-48)

And a convincing argument can be made that in Ephesus the disciples of John the Baptist got everything at once, or nearly all at once. "On hearing this, they were baptized into the name of the Lord Jesus. When Paul placed his hands on them, the Holy Spirit came on them, and they spoke in tongues and prophesied" (Acts 19:5-6).

The scriptural record urges me to hold to the need for empowerment. But I am extremely reluctant to say that it must occur in some particular order or method or style. I know this much: it takes God's power to do God's work. God works through people, yes, but he insists that his power, not ours, be the energizing force of that work.

We must, therefore, take Paul's advice to the Ephesians and "keep on being filled with the Holy Spirit" (5:18, literal translation). In the past few decades the church has been learning more and more about collaborating with the Spirit. My observation is that the Spirit interacts with us at successive levels or stages. In my own life so far there have been four major milestones of the Spirit's work: in 1972 (infilling), 1974 (anointing for inner healing), 1983 (exposure to power ministry) and 1990 (heightened commitment to prayer). Each of these levels of interaction with the Spirit renewed and refreshed me and brought significantly greater effectiveness to my ministry. It thrills me to wonder what's coming next, for as the riches of Christ are past searching out, so the ministries of the Spirit must be inexhaustible.

If you are seeking greater effectiveness in ministry, I encourage you to begin fellowshipping with the Spirit. The word *Spirit* occurs over eighty times in Paul's letters, indicating that the Holy Spirit serves and blesses believers in an astonishing variety of ways. One of those ways is fellowship: "May the grace of the Lord Jesus Christ, and the love of God, and the fellowship of the Holy Spirit be with you all" (2 Cor 13:14). Fellowship with anyone is a two-way transaction—speaking and listening. Among us humans, it seems that all too often some people only speak, some only listen. But both are necessary for fellowshipping—full sharing—to occur.

Speaking to the Spirit

What I'm going to say may sound obvious to you, but it is amazing how many Christians never think to speak to the Spirit. These are expressions I find myself frequently saying to the Spirit:

☐ "Holy Spirit, good morning! Thank you for watching over me as I slept."

☐ "Holy Spirit, this is the day the Lord has made, and you are going to help me rejoice in him."

☐ "Holy Spirit, direct my prayers to the Father as I begin my devotions this morning. Open your Word to me, and open me to your Word. Thank you."

☐ "Holy Spirit, guide my feet this day as I go about my work."

☐ "Holy Spirit, be with me as I keep this appointment with the next person I'm to meet. Let your will be done."

☐ "I bless you, Holy Spirit, for we are now going to proclaim your Word."

☐ "Holy Spirit, help me lead this meeting [service, Bible study, outreach] in your power."

☐ "Holy Spirit, help me understand what this person with me is saying. You are the go-between God, Spirit, and I know you can give me unity and understanding with this person."

☐ "I thank you, Holy Spirit, for being with me all this day. Help me relax now with my family."

☐ "Holy Spirit, guard my loved ones and me as we sleep. Refresh our bodies and spirits as we rest."

These are the kinds of things one says to a friend. Often I feel the Spirit on me as I exult, "Thank you, Holy Spirit, for being my friend."

I am hard-pressed to characterize the differences between relating with the Father, relating with the Son and relating with the Spirit, but each relationship has a distinct flavor. The Father seems awesome yet warm and reassuring to me. The Son seems natural and lordly and brotherly. And my relationship with the Spirit seems to be more operationally oriented. The Spirit is not an "it" but a "he," and I must not simply use him without relating with him, but there is a distinct sense that he is particularly interested in helping me get things done.

The habit of speaking to him naturally puts me in a frame of mind to listen to him, especially as I remind myself that I am a goner without his aid.

Listening to the Spirit

Listening to the Spirit is a very different matter from speaking to him. When I speak to him, I have only to express my own finite thoughts. But when I am listening to him, I have to hear from infinitude, which immediately catapults me into a very much wider arena. For "the Spirit searches all things, even the deep things of God" (1 Cor 2:10).

It is a radical thing to listen to God; in fact, if we did not have the Holy Spirit, we could not hear him. In that sense, listening to God is not at all natural—at least not for fallen human beings. Paul declares, "The man without the Spirit does not accept the things that come from the Spirit of God, for they are foolishness to him, and he cannot understand them, because they are spiritually discerned" (1 Cor 2:14).

Not only is God's Spirit involved in the matter of listening, so also is *our* spirit. Certainly the whole person is saved and empowered by the work of the Spirit, but the Scriptures themselves claim that parts of us are more adept at certain kinds of cooperation with God than other parts: "For who among men knows the thoughts of a man except the man's *spirit* within him?" (v. 11, my italics). The very nature of the human spirit precludes us from getting very meticulous about what it is or how it works. About the most we can say is that it was their spirits that died when Adam and Eve sinned; it's the spirit that the prophets promised would be reborn; it's the spirit that Jesus told Nicodemus had to be reborn; it's the spirit in us, reborn by the Holy Spirit, that enables us to cry to God, "Abba, Father."

To me, the most useful aspect of the spirit is that it is transrational. That is, it is able—by the work of the Holy Spirit—to apprehend truth that is beyond my mind's ability to completely understand. This is not to say that my mind is unsaved or unrenewed. It is to say that there are some functions that my mind has not been created to fulfill. The spirit is not unrational or anti-intellectual but *trans*rational: it goes further than the mind can go, especially in the matter of listening to God. God places thoughts or impressions in our minds, but it is our spirit, Paul says, that perceives or examines what those thoughts are.

Trust in the Lord is the primary quality that allows us to hear the Spirit. And the most effective way to trust is to relax. When you wish to listen to the Lord, you might say, "Holy Spirit, Jesus said we could do nothing without him, and your Word declares that spiritual matters must be spiritually discerned. So I'm going to relax, believing that you are eager to speak to me." When I do this, I tend to "dehyper." I relax physically. I relax mentally. I don't try to focus or concentrate. I may even look around in a casual or disinterested manner. Usually in a few seconds— or minutes, if I've been too intense—something comes to me. It jumps through the inner window, as it were, and I notice it.

In 1 Corinthians 12 Paul categorizes the impressions or messages that come through this window into five functions, called gifts of the Spirit. They are "the message [word] of knowledge," "the message [word] of wisdom," "prophecy," "distinguishing between spirits [discernment]" and "interpretation" (following a message given in tongues). The first four of these are often important in inner healing, so let's look at them carefully.

Word of Knowledge

A word of knowledge may be defined as the Spirit's impartation of knowledge that one has no merely human way of knowing, and that is intended to be used to benefit the person the information concerns. Tom mentioned this gift in his letter at the beginning of this chapter. These little flashes of knowledge or insight allow the Spirit to direct us into the path of healing that will most benefit the person we are ministering to.

These impressions come in a variety of ways. Some people "see" the message as if on a ticker tape, simply reading words that seem to flow across a screen in their minds. But this experience is apparently quite rare. The great majority of Christians receive input from the Spirit in one of the following ways:

☐ a picture
☐ a picture of a word
☐ an impression
☐ a spontaneous utterance of unpremeditated words
☐ a memory of something that happened to you or someone you know
☐ a concept
☐ a commonsense observation that suddenly has the force of wisdom or accuracy
☐ a sensation in your body, such as pain or heat
☐ a rush of compassion, tears or emotional pain that you know not to be your own
☐ a dream, a vision
☐ Scripture—either a reference you must look up or a passage you remember

It must be noted that these impressions are usually very slight. For years I joked that God spoke in a "whis"—half a whisper. These impressions do not bang you over the head. If you're not paying attention, you'll barely notice them. Remember, Elijah found that the Lord did not speak in the mighty wind, in the fire or in the earthquake, but in the still small voice.

Furthermore, receiving and acting on an impression from the Spirit does not "feel spiritual," whatever our stereotype of "spiritual" is. Actually, hearing from the Spirit feels entirely normal. And when you call these impressions "guidance," it *feels* as though you are lying. This fact alone accounts for most of our failures to act on guidance from God. Most people have no idea how often and how much God speaks to them. They write off the impressions they receive as quirks, mental blips, products of overactive imaginations, inexplicable cerebralisms or whatever. Usually they don't fret too much over these experiences, because they are exceedingly slight and transitory. But, as a matter of fact, they are very often the voice of God. And when we do not listen for and act on them, we waste vast amounts of the power of God.

Word of Wisdom

Another purpose in 1 Corinthians 12 for which the Spirit speaks to us is the word of wisdom. The word of wisdom can be defined as a God-given knowledge of what to do in a given situation. It is seeing through the details of a situation to the meanings, causes and ultimate purposes of those details. Often the word of wisdom encompasses a larger view and points to ultimate realities.

For example, when the Pharisees set their trap for Jesus over paying taxes to Caesar, they thought they had him in a no-win dilemma. If he said "Don't pay Caesar," they could haul him up before Pilate for fomenting insurrection; if he said "Pay Caesar," he could lose favor with the common people as a sympathizer with the hated oppressors. One way or another, they were sure the trap would work.

Jesus had said clearly that his modus operandi was to do only what he saw the Father doing. In fact, he indicated that this was not merely a choice but a necessity, for "the Son *can do nothing* by himself; he *can do only* what he sees his Father doing" (Jn 5:19). This theme is repeated at least a dozen times in John.[2] Was Jesus being humble when he said he couldn't do anything apart from the Father? I think not. Rather, I think, this was an actual description of his mode of working. He simply practiced the presence of his Father continuously and refused to act without his Father's direction.

It seems apparent, then, that when the Pharisees presented their trap, Jesus looked to the Father for direction. In a matter of seconds the Father put the wisdom in him which would resolve the matter.

> But Jesus, knowing their evil intent, said, "You hypocrites, why are you trying to trap me? Show me the coin used for paying the tax." They brought him a denarius, and he asked them, "Whose portrait is this? And whose inscription?"
>
> "Caesar's," they replied.
>
> Then he said to them, "Give to Caesar what is Caesar's, and to God

what is God's."

When they heard this, they were amazed. So they left him and went
away. (Mt 22:18-22)

On at least one occasion the word of wisdom from the Father was a bit
slow in coming. This was another trap: the case of the woman caught
in adultery (Jn 8:3-11). The Greek indicates that Jesus was quite slow
in responding, writing with his finger in the sand while they "kept on
questioning him." True to his stated mode of operating, Jesus refused
to answer out of the flesh; he waited for the Father to come through
for him.

Finally there came the word of wisdom needed to resolve the situation. "If any one of you is without sin, let him be the first to throw a
stone at her." That was all! He added nothing of his own, trusting that
this message was from the Father and that it would have its intended
effect. So he bent over and doodled in the sand again until the matter
resolved itself.

The Spirit gives the word of wisdom in the same ways as the word
of knowledge. But whereas the word of knowledge is often partial and
mysterious, the word of wisdom carries a fullness of comprehension.

A businessman recently came to my office to ask my advice on a
complicated and serious business problem. I am no businessman, but
I relaxed, focused my attention on Jesus and waited on the Spirit to tell
me what to say. Suddenly I saw the whole answer and spoke it to him
in two sentences. As he digested those words, a light came on in his
eyes and he exclaimed that that was the solution he needed. What's
more, the solution opened the way for inner healing regarding conflicts
with a partner.

In inner healing, a word of wisdom given to the team or to the person
being prayed for may indicate which memories particularly require
prayer. Pain seems to grow on "trees"; chopping down the trunk—
praying for a key memory—fells many branches, whole bunches of
other memories.

A word of wisdom may point out the real concern to be dealt with.

One of our team members kept getting the impression that he should ask the person he was ministering to about his relationship with his mother. "Oh, fine," the young man said at first. "No problem," he said next. "We have no difficulties," he said third. Finally, after being asked four times, he said, "Well, she did give me away for six months when I was three years old." The Spirit's word of wisdom pierced through his denial that there was anything to deal with in his history with his mother.

Prophecy

Paul says that "everyone who prophesies speaks to men for their strengthening, encouragement and comfort" (1 Cor 14:3). Recently I had the privilege of ministering to a dozen elders from a church in our area, none of whom I had met previously. I asked the Spirit to rest on them. Then I waited, looking at them and at the Lord.

After a few minutes I felt drawn to one older man. As I looked at him, "fatherhood" came to mind. I opened my mouth and these words came forth, "You are a father. Young men will come to you for fathering. They will receive encouragement, wisdom and protection from you. You will safeguard their ministries."

Through those few sentences, the Lord "strengthened, encouraged and comforted" that man. Then it came out that his own son was in rebellion against the Lord, and inner healing for the father's pain for his son became the agenda.

Another use of prophecy is a bit more intimidating: "But if an unbeliever or someone who does not understand comes in while everybody is prophesying, he will be convinced by all that he is a sinner and will be judged by all, and the secrets of his heart will be laid bare. So he will fall down and worship God, exclaiming, 'God is really among you!' " (1 Cor 14:24-25). During inner healing prayer, prophecy can put the finger directly on the cause of the pain of one's life. Frequently this happens when a person is not fully cooperative, refusing to disclose or acknowledge sins that need to be confessed or forgiven before healing can occur.

Discernment

The fourth purpose for which the Spirit gives guidance in inner healing is "distinguishing between spirits." Discernment, as this is also called, distinguishes between spirits that are from God and those that are not. This is important, for some people exhibit physical and emotional manifestations that may be prompted by the Spirit or by the enemy.

In a large conference in Australia, a woman began shrieking in a most disconcerting way. I was the team member closest to her, so I approached her, put my hand on her shoulder and said, "I speak peace to you." She calmed down. Then I asked if she and her husband would step into an area where we could talk, and they agreed.

As I interviewed her, I discovered that she was the wife of a pastor and had become distraught over the difficulties she and her husband were experiencing in bringing the gospel to their congregation. The Holy Spirit had put his finger on her pain, to which she responded by wailing. While her behavior had *looked* demonic, it wasn't. In short order she began to receive inner healing for feelings of discouragement, frustration and failure.

Discernment normally seems to operate as a confluence of several factors. First is knowledge of the Scriptures. The Holy Spirit will not contradict today what he inspired to be written in the Bible. When trying to assess the origin of something, we can ask, "Is this scriptural?" For example, from time to time cult groups place large ads in the newspapers. These ads often sound reasonable until they are measured against Scripture.

Second is the matter of peace. Often when the Spirit is giving discernment that something is demonic in its origin, an identifiable unrest rises up and spreads through one's chest. It may feel like a spreading emptiness of agitation. On the other hand, when the discernment is that something is of God, there is a stillness, a peace, a fullness in the center of one's chest.

Third, commonsense observation often signals to us that we may be encountering the demonic.

These three factors combine to indicate that something is of God or of the enemy or of the flesh. Taken alone, any of them could be misleading. But when found together and in agreement, they add up to discernment.

The Spirit sometimes gives discernment simply through a knowing—sometimes even a seeing—of something's spiritual origin. Some persons with this gift can actually "see" demons on people or "see" the Holy Spirit resting on someone. Often their ability to categorize what they are seeing is quite finely tuned. They may, for example, realize that someone is suffering from a spirit of religiosity that was inherited through the mother's family line.

When discernment comes, the team can pray in accordance with it. If something from the enemy is present, it can be repented of or broken or bound or expelled. If something from the Spirit is present, it can be blessed or loosed or capitalized upon by following his lead.

Listening and Obeying

The Bible is filled with stories of human beings who were explicitly guided by the Lord. Over and over when we read about David we come upon the phrase "David inquired of the Lord." God spoke very specifically to David, and the successes David enjoyed can be attributed to three actions: David listened, God answered, and David obeyed. Let's look at these three actions.

1. We listen. I have already explained that because we belong to God, we have his Spirit, and because we have the Spirit, we can hear the "things of God" (1 Cor 2:10). Part of being in communion with Father, Son and Holy Spirit is being in an inner posture of listening. The Spirit *is* within us, and he *will* speak.

As we listen for God's guidance, we need to take the attitude that God probably knows what needs to be done in every situation and we probably don't. This is reasonable, since he is infinite and we aren't. We need to come to him in childlike trust—a kind of childlikeness that Jesus himself apparently never outgrew—believing that God knows what is needed and can convey his information and wisdom to us.

2. *God speaks.* We can talk about receiving God's communications to us in terms of *listening* to what he says or *watching* what he does. I will use both kinds of verbs here, for both are useful physical metaphors for a process that happens inside us.

The first part of seeing what God is doing is passive observation. When we come to listen to the Lord, we place ourselves in a receptor mode. We are there simply to gaze on him and see what the Father is doing (Jn 5:19). At this stage we are not initiating anything except listening. We're not telling the Lord what to do; rather, we are waiting for him to tell us what to do. A concept like "practicing the presence of God" is invaluable here, for it suggests a passive, observant, trusting mode of relationship with him.

Once God communicates something, we shift to the second phase, active creation.

3. *We obey.* We Westerners have been so permeated with the values of the scientific method—objectivity, observation, verification—that we have become loath to exercise faith. "Without faith it is impossible to please God," Hebrews 11:6 clearly states. But we want to be "sure" before we take action. This desire to be sure is disastrous to the business of having faith, for faith itself is the substance and the evidence of the thing we're trying to have faith for. That is, faith stands in as the substance and the evidence of something until God gets it to us.

Active creating might be described as faith-on-the-line. It's the point at which we act on what we've seen, releasing by faith God's power to flow into the need, whether it is a memory, a physical injury, an interpersonal problem or whatever. What we do in active creating is to imagine—declare—that Jesus is actually doing the thing necessary to accomplish healing.

In that first inner healing in which I participated, I passively observed Jesus offer comfort to the woman and then remove her hurt, replacing it with healing. Once I had seen—observed—what to do, it was important to "see" it in an active way, which I did by describing Jesus doing those things and by seeing them in my active imagination.

To actively see Jesus doing something you haven't passively seen him doing is presumption. But to actively see Jesus doing something you have passively observed him doing is obedience. How to take risks of obedience without crossing into presumption can be learned only through experience. Chapter ten's summary of frequent mistakes can help you benefit from our experience and observation.

Once a sincere desire to listen to God is added to some experience-based instruction on how to listen, we will probably begin to hear from God. We can then take faithful action on what we may have heard. How can we be certain about something so elusive? We can't. But action doesn't require certainty; it requires humility, honesty and courage. God was one who invented this way of communicating, so he can be expected to help us learn it satisfactorily.

Sometimes the Spirit surprises like this: he gives an impression; we act on it; he then takes the person on his own far-reaching course without our further involvement. During the ministry time at a conference in the eastern United States, I received an impression that the Lord wanted to anoint several persons for the gift of teaching. One of those who came forward later reported the following:

I was called forward for an anointing to teach, and was overwhelmed by the Spirit, flat on the floor for about thirty minutes, really unconscious. When I came to, I got up to return to my seat, feeling a certain lightness, as if I had lost several pounds. I praised God for this experience, but the praise was just beginning. It wasn't until a week later that I realized I was not experiencing my usual lustful temptations, and that I, in fact, had absolutely no desire for pornographic stimulation of any kind. . . . What a blessing! I am still free to this day, and I just praise him for that.

A week after this, while in an inner healing session for myself, God disclosed the source experience of the demonization—a sexual molestation when I was twelve years old that had been so traumatic that I had completely blocked it from my conscious memory. I have now been healed of the pain of this memory and finally feel on my way toward freedom in Christ. Several days after this healing, I was able to *make love* to my wife (as opposed to using her for my sexual gratification) for the first time in our ten years of marriage.

Isn't that stupendous? The Spirit achieved tremendous results with only minimal cooperation from me. But I believe that if I had not listened for a word of knowledge, if I had not uttered what I thought I was hearing, if that man had not come forward in response to that word, he might still be plagued by the spirit of lust and might yet be carrying the pain that allowed the demonization to occur.

Healing

Another purpose for which the Holy Spirit inspires us in the ministry of inner healing is "gifts of healing," as 1 Corinthians puts it. That the word "gifts" is plural is instructive. I once made an actual count of the works of power that Jesus did. Seventy-seven percent of them were healings, if you include deliverance from evil spirits in that category. The other 23 percent were nature miracles. To me this indicates that healing was a mainstay of Jesus' ministry. But the plural "gifts" in 1 Corinthians 12:9 also indicates that there are many kinds of healing ministries. One person may have a special unction for healing joints, another for infections, yet another for memories and yet another specifically for the memories of abused children. That doesn't mean you cannot pray for persons with illnesses or problems outside your gift area; it simply means that you will probably be especially effective in certain areas.

For the first ten years after I was filled with the Spirit, a very high percentage of persons with joint problems were healed, but I couldn't get anyone with a cold healed. This was frustrating for me until I gained an insight that I will try to explain with the image of two hands. If I hold out my left hand and point my fingers up, each finger represents something the Lord has placed in me naturally. My thumb might represent my genetic structure, while my fingers could stand for personal history, significant experiences, natural abilities and particular interests. My right hand represents the anointing of the Spirit. It comes down, inverted, in exactly the same posture as my left to touch the tip of each finger. The spiritual gift, in other words, perfectly aligns with who I am naturally, releasing the natural gifts into an effectiveness they could never attain without spiritual enhancement. So it isn't peculiar at all that I would have spiritual gifts in certain areas and not others.

To find out what you're spiritually gifted for, my advice is that you pray for as many different kinds of persons and needs as seems reasonable to you, and see what happens. Where you seem to be effective, concentrate your energies and learn as much as you can about that area of ministry. Or the Lord may sovereignly impart a gifting to you through someone, as he did to me through Agnes Sanford.

Is there a "gift of inner healing"? I suppose there is. But the only way you can discover whether you have it is to take what you can learn from this and other books, pray in faith for people, and then examine the results. My experience is that some people are better at it than others, but everyone appreciates being prayed for. And even those who "have the gift" need to grow and develop as they use it.

12

SPIRITUAL WARFARE

Over *the years, Mike and I have felt particularly called by God to* a ministry of inner healing prayer, but we have (somewhat reluctantly) learned a great deal about spiritual warfare in the process. We have learned that inner healing prayer brings powerful defeat to the enemy by destroying his schemes and strategies to oppress and influence people. As you involve yourself in inner healing prayer, you too will discover that demonic spirits often seize a foothold in a person's life at the point where there is unconfessed sin, occult involvement, or abuse or emotional trauma from the past.

I'll never forget one of my earliest experiences of this as I prayed with Stacy (whose story is described more fully in chapter five). As I asked the Holy Spirit to be present to bless Stacy and to guide us, I noticed that Stacy was perspiring and beginning to shake.

"What's happening, Stacy?" I asked.

"I feel afraid," she answered.

I quietly took authority over any spirit of fear and bound it in the name of Jesus. As I did so, Stacy suddenly reached out to grab my throat and growled in my face: "I hate you!"

Putting my hands on Stacy's shoulders to restrain her (and trying to remain calm myself), I exercised the authority we have in Jesus and said: "Spirit of hatred, I rebuke you and bind you in the name of Jesus and command you to leave."

Within seconds, a wave of relief passed over Stacy. She fell into my arms, crying, "It's gone, it's gone!"

As we proceeded in conversation and prayer, we discovered that Stacy's idolization of her father had been blocking the authority and lordship of Jesus, exposing her to demonic attacks of fear (of losing her father) and hatred (especially toward herself as a result of her parents' divorce). Stacy repented and asked God to forgive her for making an idol of her father, for not fully trusting Jesus, and for allowing fear, anger and self-hatred to be her close companions. Through repentance and forgiveness, the enemy's ground of attack was removed.

Neither Mike nor I have desired or sought out a ministry of deliverance. But sins and weaknesses that stem from brokenness or past emotional hurts provide prime targets for the enemy's attacks, and such sins and weaknesses are what prompt people to seek inner healing. It should not be surprising, then, that we often run into demonic oppression or attachment as we pray for others—and that we need to deal decisively with the enemy's work when it is exposed. So in this chapter we will explain and seek to understand spiritual warfare in the context of a ministry of inner healing. For a more complete treatment of spiritual warfare and deliverance ministry we refer you to recent books by respected authors—Mark Bubeck, Michael Green, Charles Kraft, Francis McNutt, Peter Wagner, Thomas White and others.[1]

It's Real
The first thing we need to acknowledge is that spiritual warfare is real!

The Bible tells us that our adversary the devil wars against us. Satan tempts and attacks us in our areas of weakness and sifts us in areas of our fleshly desires.[2] Jesus refers to Satan as "the prince of this world" (Jn 14:30). In Luke 4:6 we read that the devil, showing Jesus all the kingdoms of this world, said to him, "I will give you all their authority and splendor, for it has been given to me, and I can give it to anyone I want to." John agrees that the whole world is under Satan's control (1 Jn 5:19). Satan is referred to by Paul as "the ruler of the kingdom of the air" (Eph 2:2) and by Peter as "your enemy" who "prowls around like a roaring lion looking for someone to devour" (1 Pet 5:8).

The good news of the gospel is that through Jesus—his birth, life, death, resurrection and ascension—God has invaded the realm of Satan. Jesus has overthrown Satan's rulership, bringing freedom for those enslaved to sin, sickness, demons and any other weapon the enemy has used. And those who repent, believe and accept the lordship of Jesus and follow him are liberated to participate in taking back lives that Satan has ruined and bringing them to wholeness. Christ's victory is certain (Col 2:15), but a measure of warfare continues until Christ returns in his glory.

For most of my Christian life I had avoided dealing directly with the demonic realm because of ignorance, fear and lack of experience. I wasn't sure this "warfare stuff" was real. I was under the notion—born of fear—that if I didn't bother Satan, he wouldn't bother me. Then, in early 1987, at a weekend college ministry conference at which I was the main speaker, I was given an opportunity to overcome my fear, gain the experience I lacked, and grow up more into Christ.

At the end of a lengthy evening worship service, one of the staff asked me to come to the back of the room because one of the students was behaving strangely. Jeff was on the floor, curled into a fetal position, filled with fear, unable or unwilling to answer questions or look us in the eye. With the help of the staff and three of Jeff's friends, we took him to a private room and began to pray. It quickly became apparent— much to my dismay—that everyone was looking to me to lead the prayer session. I was older, a pastor, the conference speaker and therefore the one to whom authority was most easily given. I did have some knowledge of warfare from Scripture and books, and—though I had not realized until that very moment—God had been preparing me for this experience and was giving me the boldness and authority to lead.

For the next two hours we learned about "deliverance"—breaking demonic oppression and strongholds—in the "school of the Holy Spirit." As we talked with Jeff and prayed, the Holy Spirit guided us to encourage Jeff to repent of sin patterns of unforgiveness, anger and sexual immorality. We prayed inner healing prayer for his relationships with his father and brother, who had been physically and emotionally abusive. We demanded to know, in the name and authority of Jesus, the names of any unclean spirits and what permission they had to oppress Jeff. We then rebuked and bound them in the name of Jesus and commanded them to leave. These prayers were not effective, however, until Jeff repented of his sins and removed the ground of attack from these spirits through inner healing prayer.

Then, as Jeff gained clarity about the enemy's strategy and increased faith in Jesus' power and presence, he was able to let go of unforgiveness, to give Jesus authority over his father and brother, and finally to say to unforgiveness and anger: "I don't want you anymore! I belong to Jesus. Get out! I command you to leave, in the name of Jesus!"

With this the enemy's power was fully broken, and Jeff was filled with peace. It was an incredible, joy-producing experience for all of us. Jeff seemed to warm up and turn pink ("like a newborn baby," someone commented) and shine with the presence of God. His friends fell on his neck and shoulders, hugging him in relief and gladness. And we all agreed, right on the spot, that we would be glad to do this again if such peace, joy and freedom were the outcome.

We learned that Jesus does have authority over demonic spirits, and that in his name, so do we. We learned that warfare is real, that deliverance is a part of the ministry Jesus has for us, and that he is with us to guide and protect us. We realized that Satan can't just walk into someone's life; he has to be invited in or made welcome. And this "permission" can be withdrawn. Most striking to me, I saw clearly for the first time the direct relationship between emotional brokenness and demonic oppression.

We live in a time of spiritual warfare, and we need to be equipped to fight. Inner healing prayer is one of the primary strategies God has given us to break the enemy's influence and to participate with Jesus in bringing "freedom for the prisoners" (Lk 4:18).[3]

The Foundation for Deliverance

Deliverance, briefly defined, is a process, through prayer and spiritual warfare, of freeing a person who is demonized (oppressed by evil spirits).[4] And the key to this process of deliverance is breaking and removing enemy footholds through inner healing prayer.

Francis McNutt writes that there are three basic kinds of sickness which trouble us:

☐ sickness of our spirits, resulting from personal sin, which requires prayers of repentance

☐ sickness of our emotions, resulting from trauma and emotional hurts from our past, which can be dealt with effectively through inner healing prayer and spiritual counseling

☐ sickness of the body, resulting from disease, accident and emotional stress or trauma, which can be addressed through prayers for physical healing

These sicknesses can influence each other and may be interrelated, as table 4 suggests, and they can be initiated and intensified by demonic oppression, which requires prayer for deliverance.[5]

Jeff, whose story I told above, repented for his anger, unforgiveness and sexual immorality, which had in part been a response to emotional abuse from the past. The enemy had used these areas of "darkness" as an entry in order to oppress Jeff and keep him from the things of God. Through repentance, inner healing and prayers for deliverance, Jeff was liberated to grow more into the likeness of Christ.

Table 4. Types of Healing Prayer

Condition	Contributing Factors	Prayer Action
1. Emotional sickness (often related to physical and spiritual conditions)	Sins of others Trauma/abuse Bitter root/judgment Projection Unforgiveness	Inner healing
2. Physical sickness (often related to emotional and spiritual conditions)	Disease Accident Stress	Physical healing
3. Spiritual sickness (often related to emotional and physical conditions)	Sin	Confession Repentance
4. Demonic (any of the above can be intensified by demonic oppression)	Demonic attachment	Deliverance

The real problem facing demonized people is not the demons, but the deep emotional and spiritual problems to which the demons are attached. The enemy is not creative. Satan tries to ruin and pervert the creation of God. He seeks to take advantage of the garbage (sin/trauma/brokenness) that is already there.

Charles Kraft writes: "Demonization is always secondary, just as rats are secondary to garbage. If we get rid of the rats and keep the garbage, the person is in great danger still. But if we get rid of the garbage, what we have done automatically affects the rats. *Whether there are demons or not, therefore, we go after the primary problem—the emotional and spiritual garbage.*"[6]

So deliverance is never a simple process of casting out demons. It is primarily the work of removing the spiritual sickness and emotional woundedness that has allowed the demons to enter or afflict the person in the first place. This is why inner healing is foundational for deliverance. And thanks be to God that through our union with Christ we have both authority and power to enter into this ministry—"how incredibly great his power is to help those who believe him" (Eph 1:19-20 LB).

The Enemy's Tactics

Paul cautions us not to be ignorant of Satan or his ways (2 Cor 2:11). Satan is a created being who was already defeated at Calvary by Christ; he is limited in authority, knowledge, power and presence.

☐ God has all authority. He alone is sovereign. Satan can only act within limits God has set.

☐ Only God is infinite in knowledge. Satan's knowledge is limited to information relayed to him by demons and unclean spirits.

☐ God has all power. The One who is in us is greater than the one who is in the world (1 Jn 4:4). There is limited power in Satan's name, so he bluffs, lies and deceives.

☐ Only God is everywhere. Like all created beings, Satan is never in more than one place at a time. So Satan depends constantly on demonic spirits "loyal" to him.

The enemy attacks where permission is given through human sin or where there is weakness due to emotional damage. Satan and his legions are filled with rage, envy and jealousy toward God; they seek to hinder God's purposes and ruin those who are made in God's image and able, like God, to create and love. Satan has well-rehearsed methods and strategies of oppressing people.

1. He prefers to remain hidden and keep people ignorant of his presence and influence. He attacks places of sin and emotional weakness, where there are negative tendencies, compulsive behaviors or traumatic memories. He is not creative and will use what is at hand, trying to keep us ignorant of his designs and plans. He wants us to

believe that what is happening to us is "normal" or "a part of me" or "the way I have always felt or thought."

In praying recently for Brian, we identified several "strongholds of the enemy" (cf. 2 Cor 10:4-5)—patterns of thought and experience from which the enemy could easily attack Brian and hinder his growth in Christ. One of these was a lifelong pattern of anger that gave room to spirits of anger. Brian used anger to protect himself, to take control and to walk away from challenges. He thought being an angry person was part of his nature, temperament and character. When this stronghold was exposed, Brian was able to see that he had given anger more authority to protect him than he had given Jesus. Through repentance, Brian was prepared to rebuke anger and receive the peace God promises; and through inner healing prayer and confrontation of the enemy, Brian was able to defeat the enemy's strategy. It was a revelation to him to have the enemy's work exposed and to realize that anger was not a normal and necessary part of his God-given personality.

2. If Satan cannot keep us ignorant of his tactics, if his work is exposed, then he will try to attack us through fear—fear that demons have great power, that something violent or embarrassing will happen if we try to deal with them, that they will take revenge and hurt family members and so on. All of this is a smoke screen. They have no power in relation to Jesus or to us as we exercise faith and authority through his sacrifice and shed blood. God's kingdom is advancing, and we are to be on the offensive, putting on spiritual armor and tearing down strongholds.

3. Satan acts through deceit. He is "a liar and the father of lies" (Jn 8:44). In Western culture, he deceives primarily by persuading us that he does not exist. He tries to get people to believe lies about God, others and themselves. In the Garden of Eden, his strategy was to plant doubts about God's character in the minds of man and woman. He seeks to blind "the minds of unbelievers, so that they cannot see the light of the gospel of the glory of Christ" (2 Cor 4:4). He attacks the minds of believers with "darts" of doubt and confusion about who we are and

what Christ has done for us. "You are bad," we hear in our minds, "too evil for God to accept you or forgive you. You don't deserve God's love." No! These are lies. Jesus died for us while we were still sinners (Rom 5:8). With Scripture as a "sword of the Spirit," we are to oppose all the enemy's lies.

4. Our emotions are a prime focus of the enemy's attack. Satan tempts us to hang on to negative emotions because this easily leads to sin and denial of God's will and purpose.

If I am traumatized, it is natural to have a response of fear; or if I am purposely hurt, it is natural to feel anger. But if I do not deal fully with fear or anger, it turns to sin and distrust of God and can block God's authority and healing power. Scripture commands, " 'In your anger do not sin': Do not let the sun go down while you are still angry, and do not give the devil a foothold" (Eph 4:26-27). It encourages us, "Get rid of all bitterness, rage and anger, brawling and slander, along with every form of malice. Be kind and compassionate to one another, forgiving each other, just as in Christ God forgave you" (Eph 4:31-32). It warns us not to give reign to—not to trust and depend on—worry (Phil 4:6), fear (Is 41:10) or other emotions that can block the grace of God.

5. He accuses God's people (Rev 12:10), planting thoughts and feelings of rejection, temptation or condemnation within our hearts and minds. He tries to get us to accept his condemnation as our own, using past problems, sins, failures and doubts—all of which have already been forgiven and covered by Jesus' blood—to accuse us. But the Word says, "This then is how we know that we belong to the truth, and how we set our hearts at rest in his presence whenever our hearts condemn us. For God is greater than our hearts, and he knows everything" (1 Jn 3:19-20).

Mike and I have often found ourselves attacked by the enemy in this way when we are engaged in inner healing or warfare prayer. A barrage of thoughts floods our minds—criticism, self-doubts, accusations, temptation, sexual images and so on—all designed to throw us off and cut short the ministry we are undertaking.

One day, in the midst of praying with a friend who was trapped in patterns of sexual immorality, including homosexuality, I took a break to go to the bathroom. While standing at the urinal, I had a picture in my mind of a homosexual encounter. Though homosexuality had never been a temptation for me, I was momentarily dazed and filled with self-doubt. "Why did I have that thought?" I wondered—until I realized that it wasn't *my* thought; this was an attack from the spirit of homosexuality attached to my friend. I was quickly able to refuse the thought and go on with ministry without any guilt or shame and with renewed energy and expectation of successful healing.

Satan attacks and accuses us in our minds. How free we would all be if we did not immediately believe that all our thoughts are from our own minds, and if we resisted those that do not conform to scriptural truth.

Other forms of accusation or harassment from the enemy can include being irritable; feeling fatigued; being kept from doing something you know you are to do; being critical of others and sure that the critical feelings are justified; self-pity; feeling as if circumstances and people are ganging up on you; depression; feeling rejected; feeling certain that you'll never change.

When you notice the enemy's tactic of harassment, quickly say, "Oh, it's just you. I know what you're up to. Get lost!" Be quick to "resist the devil, and he will flee from you" (Jas 4:7; 1 Pet 5:9). Tell the Lord you are relying on him to send the enemy packing; praise God; remember who God is and what he has done for you in Jesus; remind yourself that Jesus has all authority and that he triumphed over the evil one on the cross (Col 2:15).

6. Satan seeks to destroy relationships. He tries to foster gossip and animosity, envy and jealousy. The "acts of the sinful nature" (Gal 5:19-21) provide garbage for oppression, as Satan tempts us to live in self-centeredness, worry, guilt, rejection, anger, unforgiveness.

Satan wants to disrupt, hinder and confuse us. If he cannot stop us from becoming Christian, he will focus on defeating us, slowing spiritual growth, discouraging us, making us passive, keeping us from prayer and Christian fellowship. He may try to get us so busy, even in Christian activities, that we have no time to pray and grow in relationship to God. He is the destroyer of relationships. He sows disunity, disagreement, doubt and division. He revels in slander, judgmentalism, criticism and self-righteousness. His tactic is to get Christians to do his work by getting them to repeat and circulate rumors, criticism and divisive statements. In all of my church experience, this kind of attack has done more to hinder the work of the church than anything else.

7. Satan offers power, influence or other rewards. At the beginning of Jesus' ministry, Satan tempted him with magical powers, political influence and worldly authority. Jesus rejected Satan's offers by quoting the truth of God's Word. Today Satan continues this tactic, drawing people into evil by offering healing, guidance, magical powers, influence and spiritual knowledge through pagan rituals, occult involvement, spirit mediums, charms, astrology and the like.

8. Finally, if there is enough "garbage" or direct involvement in evil or occult activity, the enemy may manifest his presence directly in and through a person. If a demon is threatened or about to be discovered (as in the case of Stacy at the beginning of this chapter), or if it is strong and stupid, it may reveal itself. When manifestation comes in the context of prayer, this is usually a sign that victory is at hand.

At the end of a late-evening ministry session concluding a conference, Gene asked for prayer for what he thought was demonic oppression. As we chatted for a few minutes, I felt led to ask him, "What's the worst thing you've ever done?"

Before Gene could stop himself, he blurted out, "Bestiality!" Shame quickly colored his face. As Gene gasped for air and tried to speak, he suddenly fell to the floor. It seemed as though some force were strangling him at the throat. Kneeling over him, I bound and shut down the oppressing spirit and commanded peace in the name of Jesus.

"Do you know what is happening?" I asked Gene.

"Yes," he responded. "I have lived with this long enough and I want to be rid of it." He then told me of his secret sin and the shame and guilt that had consumed him. He laid the sin once and for all before God and received the promised forgiveness. Then he asked God to forgive him for letting the shame define him. As Gene rebuked unclean spirits of shame and bestiality, commanding them to leave in the name of Jesus, they left with loud groans and convulsive shudders.

Then Gene leaped to his feet and did a little dance of joy for the victory he had won in Jesus. And I danced with him!

Jesus said that his authority to drive out demons was proof that the kingdom of God was already present (Lk 11:20). And he gave this same authority to his followers—first to his apostles and then to the seventy-two—"power and authority to drive out all demons and to cure diseases" (Lk 9:1; see also 10:1, 18-20). He told his disciples to teach others to obey everything he had commanded (Mt 28:20) and that those with faith in him would be able to do similar works, even greater works than he did (Jn 14:12). As the Father sent Jesus, so Jesus appoints and sends us (Jn 15:16; 20:21) to speak and act with authority in his name.

What to Do (How to Get Rid of Demons)

As Mike and I pray for people, we know we are engaged in spiritual warfare—taking back the enemy's territory and canceling his ground of attack. We aren't looking for demons, but we know that where strongholds of sin exist, or where emotional damage has created unhealthy patterns of defense or response, these have provided invitation for demonic attack. So we expect to run into demons, and when we do we are prepared with scriptural truth and with tactics that are in line with God's Word and refined through personal experience. These are some of the steps we keep in mind as we proceed in inner healing prayer.

1. How strong is the demonic attachment? If a demon manifests in some way during the prayer session—for example, by creating panic or fear, by distorting the person's face or by speaking to the person's mind or through his voice—or if you strongly suspect demonic influence because the person's will seems paralyzed or she is afraid of God or the things of God, then address what is there and take authority over it in the name of Jesus. Basically, this means shutting it down until you are ready—under God's guidance—to command it to leave. Declare that it cannot hurt the person or anyone else present and that it cannot disrupt the prayer process. Remind the person (and yourself) that you are under God's protection.

In *Defeating Dark Angels* Chuck Kraft has a helpful "Strength of Attachment Scale."[7] On a scale of 1 to 10, demons with a level 1-2 attachment are weak and can do little more than harass the person. At a level of 3-4 they can cause uncontrollable anger and fear and speak to the person's mind or, if the person allows, through the person's voice. At higher levels there are obvious compulsive sins and seeming paralysis of the person's will (5-6) or direct subjection to the enemy through occult activity (7-8). For more detail, consult Kraft's book.[8] It is important to remember that it is not the strength of the demon but the strength of the attachment that is important. So the first strategy is to weaken the demon by removing the attachment through repentance and renouncing false allegiances and through inner healing—"removing the garbage." When weakened, the demons can be defeated and cast out with no violent struggle or harm done to the person.

2. *What permission does it have?* Ask the Holy Spirit to bring to the person's mind (and to the minds of those praying) any ground or permission the enemy may have to oppress through sin, emotional damage or influence in the generational line. Almost always as we pray and ask for such guidance—even demanding to know what is there in the name of Jesus—words will quickly come: "anger," "lust," "adultery."

A few days ago, praying for Janine, as I asked the Holy Spirit if the enemy had any attachment, I received a strong impression of the word *worry.*

"Are you worried about anything?" I asked Janine.

"No, nothing I can think of," she responded. I asked her what was happening in her life, and she spoke of recent academic failures that she had not been able to share with her parents out of fear of their disapproval (in a time when they were undergoing financial hardships) and her resulting depression and immobility.

"And you aren't worried?" I questioned.

As we talked, she saw that worry, fear and anxiety had been such constant companions that she was deadened to their presence. She wanted to be rid of these things and sense God's closeness. We were quickly on our way—through repentance and applying scriptural truth—to breaking the enemy's attachment.

The key to deliverance is finding what permission the enemy has to oppress, and then to go after that—following Jesus our liberator's lead—to weaken and eventually drive away the afflicting spirits.

3. The person's will is crucial. It is not wise to move forward in prayer beyond where a person is willing and desiring to go. If they are afraid or confused, it is important to stop and deal with their feelings. Ask, "Why are you afraid?" Then take time to build faith, explore what Scripture says, be reminded of the goodness of God, acknowledge that his love casts out all fear and so forth. When a person understands what is happening—that there may be an enemy stronghold or attachment, as with Janine above—and wants to proceed, placing trust in God, then move forward.

Most, if not all, successful deliverance involves exercise of the person's will—saying no to the enemy's influence, repenting of sin, refusing any more cooperation with the enemy's lies—and, taking authority in Jesus' name, commanding the demonic spirit to leave. Chuck Kraft believes "there are three keys to deliverance: God's power, the person's will, and getting rid of the garbage the demons cling to in the person. Demons will do their best to weaken the person's will because they know they cannot stand against a human will that's set against them."[9]

4. Once the demons are weakened, it can be helpful to challenge them directly. When they are weak they cannot squirm away, bluff or lie as easily, and you can gain information to confirm what is happening. Be sure this is all right with the person receiving prayer. Remember: go only as far as he or she is willing. Explain to the person that you can't be sure what strength or foothold the enemy may still have and ask if he or she is willing to find out. Speak to what you expect might be there—for example, a spirit of lust, or despair, or anger. Command it out of hiding, and to attention, in the name of Jesus.

The answer may come to the mind of the person being prayed for, or through his or her voice if the attachment is still strong. Remember that in Jesus you have authority over any demons and they must answer. This may take some time, so be persistent and insistent.

If any demons are present, ask for their names and what permission they have to be there. As you gain information, continue to weaken the demons by removing footholds through prayers for inner healing, repentance for unconfessed sin, renouncing intergenerational spirits or any curses or pronouncements, or whatever is needed.

In one difficult case, after several hours of prayer—mostly inner healing for emotional abuse and incest—there was still a definite demonic presence in Sandra. She had a picture in her imagination of an ugly creature, passive, unmoving and unconcerned. It would not give its name or provide any information, and we were stalemated, grasping for direction. On impulse, I asked Sandra what she would call it if she had to give it a name.

"I don't know," she said, "but it sure is stubborn."

At that Sandra's two friends, sitting on either side of her, sat bolt upright and said in unison, "You are the most stubborn person we know!"

"I am stubborn . . ." Sandra responded. And then: "Oh, this is big."

I took authority over a spirit of stubbornness and commanded it out of hiding. Sandra felt its grip in her stomach and saw in her imagination that its face suddenly bore a look of panic.

And then the battle was on. Was Sandra willing to give up stubbornness—which she had relied on to protect her and keep her out of the control of others, especially men—and let Jesus be her protection instead? Was she willing to trust Jesus and give him authority over the stubbornness that had ruled her life?

It took some time for Sandra to will to do this, but as she finally repented of holding on to stubbornness and robbing Jesus of his proper authority, the demonic foothold was broken and Sandra saw Jesus with her in the picture, advancing on "stubbornness" to destroy it. With her human will set against stubbornness, and with Jesus at her side, Sandra was more than the demon could face. Sandra saw him flee with a terrified scream, and the victory was won.

5. When there is no more permission for demons to remain and the footholds are removed, bind the demons and cast them out in Jesus' name. Let the person you are praying for command them to the pit or to the feet of Jesus to do with as he wishes. Ask Jesus to show the person in some way that this is happening (as with Sandra), and wait for confirmation. You can have the most confidence that deliverance is completed when the person sees or senses in some manner what Jesus is doing and that the victory is won.

Often Jesus will be present with the person in a powerful way, giving affirmation of his love and purpose. Take time during the process to deal with any more "garbage" that comes up; trust the Holy Spirit to be a faithful guide for what needs to happen.

6. Fill the cleansed places with Jesus' love, peace and blessing. Ask and wait for Jesus to touch the person in the places that were wounded. Pray protection for the ground that has been gained. Pray for quickness in repenting of new sin and strength to resist further attacks. Bless the person with what has been missing—confidence and courage if there has been fear, peace and love if there has been anger, self-love and acceptance if there has been self-hate.

7. Give postprayer counsel. People must be willing to change their habits, patterns, thinking and whatever else is necessary to continue the healing and freedom God has given. Returning to old patterns or failing to build new ones can open the door for further oppression.

Help people begin new patterns by suggesting study of Scripture that will reinforce the new understandings (and that can then be used as a sword of the Spirit). Take them through Ephesians 6:10-20 as an example, showing them how to "put on the armor of God" so they can stand against the devil's attacks. Challenge them to put on the armor daily. Encourage them toward supportive Christian fellowship and recommend warfare prayers that can be prayed for the next few weeks,[10] and give other encouragement the Spirit brings to mind.

I usually spend time helping the person understand that the enemy has been lying to her about who she really is. She is "in Christ" (many references), called his "friends" (Jn 15:15), set apart to become like Jesus (Rom 8:29), chosen by Jesus (Jn 15:16) and empowered by him (Lk 9:10). In Jesus we have power and authority to "move mountains" (Mk 11:23-24), "bind things on earth" (Mt 18:18) and ask whatever we will in his name and he will give it (Jn 15:7, 16). These are incredible promises from a loving Father and gracious Lord that will be fulfilled in the lives of those who are fully submitted to him. All things are possible for those who believe (Mk 9:23).

Forward in Battle
We end this chapter with a word of encouragement. Jesus has won! And we are part of a mighty army following him into victory. With Jesus, by the Holy Spirit, we are given authority to attack Satan's territory, demolish his arguments, confront any opposition and destroy it by spiritual weapons. "Though we live in the world we are not carrying on a worldly war," writes Paul, "for the weapons of our warfare are not worldly but have divine power to destroy strongholds. We destroy arguments and every proud obstacle to the knowledge of God, and take every thought captive to obey Christ" (2 Cor 10:3-5 RSV). Chief among the weapons we have is inner healing prayer.

Stand up to the devil, and he will turn from you and run (Jas 4:7). The Greek word for "stand up" means to "come to stand against," to oppose. This command to stand, resist or oppose is as much a command as the command to witness or preach or heal. The world is a battleground, and we are to be warriors for Christ. Jesus' death was not only to deliver us from our sins but to empower us so that we can defeat

Satan and enforce Jesus' victory through prayer warfare.

So let us burn with the fire of holy desire to expose the falsehoods of Satan. Let us push aside the mountains Satan has thrown up against God's will and free all Satan's captives. To God be the glory!

13

WIDER DIMENSIONS OF INNER HEALING

One *of God's mind-stretching characteristics is his fascinating com-* bination of changelessness and change. He himself never changes; he is "the same yesterday and today and forever" (Heb 13:8). In that immutability we take great confidence: the God we approached yesterday is going to be just as approachable today. But his Word also declares that he is always doing a new thing. The Changeless One effects change constantly.

Already this book may have significantly changed your awareness of what God is up to these days. But in this chapter we wish to discuss some signs that portend a yet wider divine work in current affairs than many of us have anticipated before.

Inner Healing *in* the Corporate
Throughout this book we have emphasized inner healing ministry with

one person at a time. Yet there are ways to heal people in group settings as well. A leader who is sensitive to the promptings of the Holy Spirit can wrap whole categories of persons under the healing wing of the Spirit at once. One such "generic" healing prayer might go like this:

Holy Spirit, I ask you now to remind each person present of some childhood hurt experienced at their primary school. Bring to mind such an event, Lord. (Pause)

Now, Lord, let each person here remember what happened. Let each one "run the tape" of memory. And let each one remember the feelings that the event produced in them. (Pause)

Now Lord, as though the event has just occurred, approach this person who has been hurt. Put your arms around them. Tell them that you understand their pain and that you feel it with them. Comfort them with the physical touches that are appropriate to their age and personality. (Pause)

Next, Lord Jesus, I ask you to deal with their pain. You may reach right inside their heart and take it from them. You may simply announce that it won't negatively affect them anymore. You may comfort them so richly that it disappears of its own accord. Whichever way, Lord, counteract their pain. (Pause)

Lord, I invite you to speak words of encouragement, acceptance and endearment to them now. Let their minds hear the words you're using. (Pause) When it seems that the healing is full, send them on their way again, Lord Jesus.

Many people have received very significant dimensions of inner healing in a format such as this. I (Mike) once felt led to pray for all the women present who had never had a date in their college years. In those few moments several lives were changed. At other times the Lord has led me to pray in group settings for marriage blow-ups, for rejections and disappointments on the job, for those whose lives were disrupted by accidents, for all those who had experienced sexual trauma in their adolescent years. I have always been amazed at what God has accomplished in group settings.[1]

Inner Healing *of* the Corporate

God can do inner healing *in* the corporate, and he can do healing *of* the corporate. In fact, God sees us as corporate to a much greater extent than we Westerners realize or desire. Noticing this in Scripture some years ago, I began calling this factor the "dynamic of communality."[2] The dynamic of communality is a responsibility for one another, an accountability to one another, a causal linkage with one another, and a fate-sharing that is very common in Scripture but contrary, even loathsome, to our Western individualistic worldview. Whether we like this view of humans or not seems incidental to God. He sees things as he sees them, and he's not likely to change his viewpoint.

Again and again Scripture shows that people are banded together and corporately responsible.

☐ Seven of Saul's sons are killed because Saul broke faith with the Gibeonites. Then "God answered prayer in behalf of the land" (2 Sam 21:3-14).

☐ Contrary to the will of God, King David takes a census. Seventy thousand Israelites perish in a plague as punishment for David's act; note that to God this seems fair (2 Sam 24).

☐ The angel of the Lord kills 185,000 Assyrian soldiers because their general insulted the God of the Israelites (2 Kings 19:35).

☐ The sins of the fathers are visited upon the children to the third and fourth generations (Jer 32).

☐ The whole country of Moab is judged because it will not go off into exile with the Israelites (Jer 48:11).

☐ "In Adam all die" (1 Cor 15:22).

This communality is not only negative but also positive:

☐ God promises blessing to all peoples because of Abraham's faithfulness (Gen 12:3).

☐ God spares punishment to some of the later kings because of his promises to David (for example, in 2 Kings 8:19).

☐ The *friends* of the paralytic have faith that enables Jesus to heal him (Mt 9:2).

☐ To welcome a child in Jesus' name is to welcome Jesus himself (Mt 18:5).
☐ Likewise, to minister to the poor is to minister to Jesus and receive a reward (Mt 25:40).
☐ "In Christ all will be made alive" (1 Cor 15:22).

What I am suggesting is that God views us humans as bound together, for good and for ill. We can cause each other great harm or great blessing. When Nehemiah repented, he said, "I confess the sins we Israelites, including myself and my father's house, have committed against you" (Neh 1:6). He owned the sins of his forebears and confessed them as his own. Daniel had the same mindset, confessing the sins of his people as his own for fifteen verses: "we have sinned," "we have not listened to your servants the prophets," "we are covered with shame," "we have rebelled" (Dan 9:4-19). And while there isn't a single first-person singular ("I" or "me") reference in the Lord's Prayer, there are nine first-person plural references: "our . . . us . . . we." Is this merely the liturgical "we," or can it be that Jesus had in mind that we confess the sins of others as well as our own when he told us to pray, "Forgive us our debts"? Daniel did.

Finally, there is a growing body of scriptural and observable evidence that this connectedness has vertical as well as horizontal dimensions. Pieter Bos, associated with YWAM in Holland and leader of the Amsterdam City Prayer Movement, tells how an interdenominational group conducted a prayer walk to the former headquarters of the Dutch East India Company to publicly confess the sins of this company in the former colony of the East Indies, now Indonesia. Two Moluccan (East Indonesian) participants, both mature Christians and fully integrated into the Dutch culture, came under the power of the Holy Spirit on opposite sides of the area, sobbing uncontrollably as long as the confessions were being made. Finally they stood up, independently testifying that they had been healed of their fear of the white man, of which neither had been previously aware.

Here we see that inner healing can occur at corporate levels, bridging great leaps of space and even of time, bringing the power of God down upon our corporate heads.

A number of current leaders in inner healing are proposing that representations of the whole can successfully address groupwide spiritual conditions. For example, John Dawson tells of two hundred frustrated street evangelists who could induce no one to accept their tracts or testimonies in the Argentine city of Córdoba. They spent a day fasting, discerning and repenting for the sin of pride in that area. Then they humbled themselves publicly. That broke open the resistance to the gospel, allowing many hundreds of Argentines to come to the Lord over the next period of the evangelistic outreach.[3]

In various places pastors are experimenting with being "the elders at the gate" of their city, repenting for the city's sins and blessing the city's benefits. Significant spiritual breakthroughs seem to be attending these experiments.

I have had the deep honor of participating in a pastors' prayer gathering since the spring of 1989. A couple of years ago, the Presbyterian congregation across the street from us was experiencing great pain related to the firing of a staff person. During one weekly prayer gathering we clergy prayed for the pastor of that flock. Then the Holy Spirit did something wonderful.

The next Sunday I told my congregation that we were going on a "sneak attack of love." We quickly crossed the street en masse, jammed into their narthex and, at a signal, walked into the sanctuary, surrounding the people. I asked the pastor, who knew we were coming, if I could take the microphone. Then I told my people to extend a hand toward the Presbyterian congregation and sing this song to our brother and sister Christians:

I will change your name
You shall no longer be called
Wounded, outcast, lonely or afraid.
I will change your name,
Your new name shall be

Confidence, joyfulness, overcoming one,
Faithfulness, friend of God,
One who seeks my face.

We sang it through twice. Then I prayed a prayer of healing and blessing over the people and the pastor. Last, I instructed my people to "hug someone on your way out." As they say, there wasn't a dry eye in the place. When we got back across the street to our own building, our people were really jazzed, gleefully rubbing their hands together and asking if we could "do it" to another church.

Over the next few weeks a stream of notes, letters, phone calls and visits came to us from the Presbyterians across the street. Finally, at one of the pastors' prayer gatherings, their pastor declared that they were "healed of the hurt" and able to resume their journey forward. God had used a mere ten-minute visit of our flock to help heal that whole congregation. That's what I mean by inner healing of the corporate.

Whom do you represent? Of what groupings are you a part? Daniel could confess the sins of the Israelites because he was an Israelite and because God had appointed him for that task.

What is your family's self-image? What seems to be the personality of your denomination? Does your city have a fairly strong or a fairly weak view of itself? Who birthed you, baptized you, ordained you, listens to you, taxes you, calls you their own? These are your groupings. As a representative of your family or denomination or city, how about asking God if you can pray—especially with others—for the healing of your groupings?

But be very cautious about trying to represent groups of which you are not, in fact, a part. God is the God of all groupings, and he can appoint whom he wills for particular tasks, but it seems that he usually appoints as representatives those whom the groups themselves recognize as their own. It might be arrogance to confess the sins of a nation that is not your own, whereas it might be humility to confess your nation's sins against that other nation. Leave it to one of their own to confess their sins.

Singing the Lord's Song

In chapter one, as I wrote the story of how I became involved in the ministry of inner healing, I fervently hoped that you, the reader, would forget about the weird aspects—head-bobbing, "anointing" and so on—and just receive the teachings this book provides. Now I find myself forced to describe yet another weirdness, and I again hope you won't bail out on me—or on the Lord.

When the Lord directed me to write about "singing the Lord's song," I complained. I mentioned credibility. He said, "What credibility is worth anything unless it's from me?" I complained of embarrassment. He reminded me that he made Isaiah walk naked for three years as a demonstrated sermon to the Egyptians. *That* was embarrassment! I rejoined that I'm no Isaiah. He responded that, apart from him, Isaiah was no Isaiah. I went back to credibility. He spoke of obedience. I recalled a time I took some flak for this from leaders I respect. He nodded and glanced at his hands, and I was ashamed to complain about flak.

So I proceed. Read the following with whatever lenses God has given you.

In the mid-eighties, I attended a conference at which Francis MacNutt sang a song to fifteen hundred people. The song was in a language given by the Spirit. While it went on—about five minutes—I was analyzing it so much that I received no benefit from it. But I was scheduled to join Francis right after the meeting to pray for anyone who would come up.

Just as we were looking over the site assigned for prayer, a woman ran up to Francis in complete unselfconscious joy, declaring that an egg-sized tumor on the side of her neck had totally disappeared while he was singing. *That* got my attention. But I wrote it off as a peculiar gift of Francis's, certainly never suspecting that I would ever do such a thing.

A year later I was leading a small midweek worship service when the Lord reminded me of what Francis had done. Then, at considerable impact to my adrenaline gland, he said, "You do it!"

"Aw, Lord, there you go asking me to do something foolish again."

Silence.

"But Lord, I've never done that before."

Silence.

I knew that if I pondered it very much, I'd chicken out. And the twenty or so people were just looking at me, wondering why I wasn't doing or saying anything. So I told them to relax, close their eyes—I didn't want them staring at me—and expect that God was going to bless them in some way while I, uh, sang to them in the name of the Father.

I then sang for about six minutes. As I sang each line, I would hear the next one in my mind. I sang words and tunes I had never heard before. When I thought it should end, I looked at the people. Each one was "deep in the Spirit." What do I mean by that? Well, each looked as though he or she might be asleep. None moved. All looked exceedingly peaceful. Some had tears in their eyes. The atmosphere was pregnant with quietude.

I didn't have the courage to ask them what had happened. I felt lucky that I had survived another weirdness, and I fervently hoped I wouldn't be required to do that again.

Fat chance! Since then, I suppose I've sung songs like that forty or fifty times. Each time the song is different. Each time people go into deep peace. Each time a few people come to me afterward and tell me what happened to them. For most it was an inner healing. But the Spirit is not limited to inner healing: once a man's scoliosis was straightened during the song; another time a pastor declared that he was delivered of a spirit of homosexuality; many proclaimed that they simply felt the loving presence of God.

What's the scriptural explanation for this? Francis MacNutt calls it "the Lord's song," but when I looked up that phrase in Scripture, I found that it refers to a song *to* the Lord rather than one *from* him. One hint is Romans 8:26, where Paul says the Spirit "intercedes for us with groans that words cannot express." My sense is that while I sing the Holy Spirit makes intercession out of those words, and the Father responds by touching each person present in some appropriate way.

But another Pauline passage, 1 Corinthians 12:10, says that the Spirit gives "to another speaking in different kinds of tongues, and to still another the interpretation of tongues." There is almost never an out loud interpretation when I sing this song. I was bothered about that until it occurred to me that the Lord gave a message to each individual and interpreted it by the result that occurred to or in each one individually.

Recently I sang to about six hundred persons in a conference. All but a handful indicated that they had experienced a significant visit from the Holy Spirit. The next day, several stated that the presence of the Lord was still with them powerfully. When I interviewed them, they spoke of enormously different results, yet the blessing hand of the Lord was apparent to and in each.

I must confess that much of this is a mystery to me. I keep learning more about what God does in this, but very slowly. I have had to confront my preferred way of operating: must I understand the things of God before I can use them, or can I use them when it seems that the Spirit is leading and hope for understanding later? My preference is the former; God's choice sometimes seems the latter. Were there not fruit, I would abandon the practice immediately. But every time God has led me to do this foolish thing, the great majority of those present speak or give other evidence of blessing.

Now I must ask *you:* will you do what you become convinced the Lord wants you to do? Are faulty understanding, embarrassment, image and "we've never done this before" sufficient reasons to fend off the will of God? Before I move on, let me tell you one more story.

A pastor who does considerable counseling brought to my office a woman who had been so badly abused in her youth that she was terribly bound up emotionally. She had not shed a tear since adolescence. The first time I prayed for her there was no discernible result. When the pastor called a couple of weeks later asking to bring her again, I quailed inwardly: "Why? What good will it do?" But he persisted, so in they came again.

This time I listened hard for guidance from the Lord, and the impression that came was "Sing the Lord's song to her." So I told her I was going to sing her a lullaby from God the Father and asked her to relax and close her eyes. She agreed.

I began to sing softly in tongues. After a minute, she began to weep. So I sang for eight or ten minutes. And as long as I sang, she wept.

You see, the arm of the Lord is never short. Through that simple song he found the chink in her armor against him, moved through and began touching the areas of pain that she had blocked off from herself and others and God. Her pastor continued for weeks afterward to pray for her healing in the matters the Spirit had opened up.

Inner Healing as Intercession

A parishioner came to my office, complaining that nothing she said or did made any difference in her husband's refusal to come to church. I didn't know how to respond to that, so I asked the Lord what to do. It came to my mind to pray for inner healing for the husband. When I asked her if any Christians had hurt him, she responded that a supposedly devout aunt had cheated him quite badly.

For a couple of minutes we prayed a simple prayer of inner healing for him, asking Jesus to take away the pain and enable him to forgive his aunt and realize that Jesus was not responsible for his aunt's sin against him.

The next Sunday that husband was in church, and the Sunday after that he fully gave his life to Jesus.

Over the past twenty years my family and I have often taken strangers into our home. One young man—I'll call him David—lived with us for about seven weeks. When he first arrived, he was so paranoid that the sounds of traffic frightened him. He wouldn't mow the grass with the power mower for fear of the engine's noise. He refused to give us his full name and wouldn't even tell us what state he was from.

A couple of days after his arrival I took a drive into the mountains, and as I drove I prayed for various concerns. When David came to mind, I said, "Lord, how can I pray for David?"

"Pray inner healing for him," came the reply.

"For *what?*" I rejoined, somewhat sarcastically. "He hasn't told us anything that we could pray for."

"What would you *guess* would put a young man in that condition?"

So for about forty-five minutes I simply made up events in a twenty-year-old's life and prayed inner healing for them as though they had actually occurred.

The next day David came into my office. "Do you mind if we talk?" he asked. Over the next hour I was stunned as he gave an account of the very events I had prayed about the day before. What had seemed to be my making things up was actually guidance from the Holy Spirit.

David's traumas had been significantly dealt with in that intercession, so that he was freed to begin discussing his problems and working toward greater health. By the time he left us, he was far down the road to well-being.

Inner Healing as Evangelism

Our church is located within two blocks of the downtown area of Burbank. It is common for street people and homeless to come into the office for aid. One homeless fellow barged past my secretary and into my office in full midparagraph ire at God for the problems he'd been having.

After a couple of minutes I induced him to sit down. Then I said, "What's this about a workbench?"—for the Lord had brought one to mind.

He looked as though I'd slapped him, and then tried to act as if it meant nothing. But I persisted. Finally his anger cooled enough for him to explain that he'd been on the street for seven years, that he had a seven-year-old son for whom he had desperately wanted to buy a workbench for Christmas, that he'd never been able to save enough money to buy it, and that this failure caused him volumes of grief.

"Let's ask God to heal you of that hurt."

"God can't do that!"

"Yes he can."

"Why should he? I'm mad at him!"

"He loves you anyway, whether you're mad or not."

At last he let me pray for him. God touched his hurt with his generous, gracious mercy. Then I was able to help him a bit on the financial end. And he left.

The next Sunday he slipped into the back pew after the service had started. He left before it ended, and I never saw him again. I don't know if he gave his life to Jesus or not. But I know that the Lord used a simple inner healing prayer to reach out to him with hard-to-resist tenderness and love. I know our time together was one of the invitations by which the Lord will bring that man to himself for salvation, recovery and a new manner of life.

Inner Healing and Reconciliation

Perhaps you recall the girl in chapter one, whose father was emotionally distant because his mother had died when he was a child. The girl was healed and reconciled to the memory of her father, partly because she saw that her father had been so wounded. As she saw the reasons for his emotional distance—and as she saw that *she* was not the cause of those reasons—she was more able to understand him, forgive him and accept him as he was. Inner healing often brings reconciliation.

One day I was sitting across the room from a man who had come into my office to seek help for personal problems. His sins, which he confessed, disgusted me. I was trying to figure out how to muster up an attitude of gentleness toward him when the Lord burst into my consciousness with this statement: "A sin is an illegitimate means of filling a legitimate need."

As I digested that, I realized that this man's sins, disgusting as they were, were but his misguided, self-reliant, uninformed, even desperate attempts to fill the ache in his heart. That realization turned me toward him. I expressed a gentleness that was real and a compassion that led him to hope for some blessing from God. And God did indeed forgive him and then heal him of the ache he had tried to assuage with sin.

What's more, he and I became reconciled. The mention of his sins had alienated us, but the Lord's perspective on his sins and the healing of his hurts brought us together.

I have prayed for women who had been raped. Their inner healing has helped them become reconciled to the male half of the race. In the same way, racial, economic, cultural and social alienations are being addressed effectively with inner healing prayer. Inner healing is not the only kind of prayer for these concerns, but it is one effective kind.

When I was first learning the ministry of inner healing, a woman contacted me from a city far away, asking if she could fly to Los Angeles and see me. I agreed. When we met, she confessed that she and her father had aborted her child many decades before. Then she said that they had dissected the body out of scientific curiosity. I was shocked, but managed to pray for her inner healing anyway.

But at home that night, I found that I could not find sleep. I kept hearing her say that they had dissected her baby, and I kept thinking of my own sons. Each loop of those thoughts made me more appalled at what she had done. After many hours of tossing and turning, I finally cried out to the Lord. Then I realized that *I* needed inner healing from hearing about such a tragedy. So I prayed that Jesus would go back a few hours and be with me in the room where I ministered to the woman, put his arm around my shoulders as I heard those terrible words, and reach into my heart to take away the pain and shock they had caused, replacing them with his healing and reassurance.

Later he did more. He used that event and its healing to bring me into a greater understanding of and gentleness toward women who seek abortions and those who perform them. I have become reconciled not to their act but to their persons, not to their sin but to their need. Without inner healing I believe I would have harbored bitterness, judgment and a coldness of spirit that would have kept any of these people from finding mercy or healing through me.

Some time after that, a pastor friend disclosed that he and his wife found themselves with an unplanned pregnancy. One option they were considering was abortion. I felt led to say with great gentleness that the Lord probably had another plan in mind, but I did not lecture or threaten him.

A month later we met again. He told me that he and his wife had decided they could not go through with an abortion, but that they were now grieving because she had spontaneously miscarried.

As I checked in with Jesus, the Spirit of the Lord rose up in me and I commanded him, "Tell me the sex of the child!"

He answered, "Oh, we didn't have time to even think of its sex, and it was too young to tell."

"You know the sex of that child," I said. "Tell me now."

Suddenly he choked up with recognition. A few moments later, when he was able to speak, he said, "It was a boy."

"Now tell me the name of this boy."

"Oh, we hadn't even begun to think of names."

"You have a name for that boy in you. Tell me what it is."

"Timothy," he said a few seconds later.

"Father," I prayed, "we ask you to receive Timothy to your bosom. We ask you to put that name on him. We ask you to reach into his little heart and heal him of the trauma of having been miscarried. We ask that you give him eternal life with you in the heavens. We ask that you enable him to grow up at your knee and greet his mother and father when they join him. Amen."

My friend later reported that he and his wife walked in glory for weeks because of what the Lord had done in that prayer. *Love never fails!*

An Ever-Creative Lord

The interaction between the Spirit and the Word which we have experienced in our ministries of inner healing leads us to expect that the Lord will continually find new applications of the truths, graces and methods he has revealed to his church. His creativity is boundless, yet he is faithful to his Word and his promises. As the church learns to saturate itself in Scripture and to practice on-the-spot intimacy with the Spirit of the Lord, we expect that people like you will be teaching people like us what new things the Spirit is doing in the years ahead.

May the Lord use what we have written to lead you toward your own inner healing. And now that you have learned much of the theology, dynamics and methods of inner healing, perhaps he will guide you into this ministry for others. Experience, trust and continued reading will help you find the techniques as they are needed.

An unlimited reservoir of the grace of God waits to flow out to hurting people. Are you eager to be used by him in this ministry? God is even more eager to use you. Humbly go bold.

Appendix

MARSHA'S STORY

The following experience—of Marsha—happened at the Urbana missions conference in December 1990. Because it is fairly lengthy, and recounted here from two points of view, we decided to include it as an appendix. It is extremely helpful in demonstrating how inner healing can unfold, and the two perspectives—first from Betsy Lee, a member of the Prayer Ministry Team we led at Urbana, and then from Marsha herself—give further testimony to the complexity of our inner emotional issues, the power of guidance from the Holy Spirit and the incredible love and mercy of Jesus.[1]

From Betsy Lee
Urbana 90 was an incredible experience for the Prayer Ministry Team. Jesus was among us, touching and healing, restoring wholeness and hope. When I think back over those dramatic days of ministry, I see a series of faces in my mind's eye: tear-stained, tormented faces transformed into beautiful faces that shone with radiance and joy. As one team member said seeing those faces, "They had freedom written all over them." No individual experience was more moving to

me than the deep inner healing that Marsha received.

After a teaching on sexuality, Mike Flynn, the director of the ministry team, asked for the Holy Spirit to fill the room. He then instructed members of the Prayer Ministry Team to circulate among the crowd, touching and blessing what the Holy Spirit was doing in individual hearts. Tears came as sin and hurt began to surface.

My attention was drawn to a young woman who was sitting on a step, sobbing with her head buried in her hands. I could not tell if she was a woman or a man when I first looked at her. She had close-cropped hair, wore no makeup and was dressed in jeans and tall black boots. She was older than the rest of the students, perhaps in her late thirties. She had been a Christian for six months.

I asked her if someone on the ministry team had prayed for her. Yes, she said, someone had. I put my arm around her, then I drew closer and looked into her eyes, walling out the distraction of eight hundred people in the room. I asked if she needed more prayer. She smiled through the tears—a very gentle, sweet smile—and nodded.

I sat down beside her on the step, putting my arm around her and holding her close. She began to tell me her story, and I assured her that healing was a process. It would take time, years probably, before she was completely healed, but Jesus who had begun a good work in her would complete it. "God will make you whole," I said.

When I said these words, her eyes grew wide. She seemed surprised. I didn't think that much about it; the conversation went on.

Later she explained that when I had found her sitting on the step after the one team member had left, she had been in the presence of the Holy Spirit, really not knowing what to do next. "I kept hearing the words *I am going to heal you. I will make you whole,*" said Marsha. "Then you came up to me and used those exact words."

Marsha cried and told me she really couldn't believe God could love her. She felt worthless, unlovable. "I have no friends," she said. "I feel untouchable."

I told her that Jesus broke all the norms of society by touching lepers, who were literally called "untouchables" in his day. I gently pressed my hand on her shoulder as I said: "When Jesus reached out and touched a leper, it must have been a more powerful statement than all the sermons he preached." Sometimes, I explained, it's not enough to hear the words "God loves you"; you need to feel it, tangibly receive his touch.

Marsha smiled a big smile. She patted my hand and drew me closer. "Yes," she sighed. "Yes. That is what I feel now—as if your hand is his hand."

Then she told me why she felt untouchable. Marsha had been sexually abused by her mother at the age of two. It was not a single incident, but a repeated trauma. She had never known a father. She was also sexually abused by her sisters. As she grew up, she was promiscuous, going from man to man. Now she was celibate. "I don't believe a man can like me for who I am."

I listened to Marsha's pain, feeling great compassion, but detached too because I take the Lord's place as I minister, and I usually do not enter into the tears of the other person. But what Marsha told me next was unbearable. It completely shattered my reserve.

"You can't believe what they did to me," said Marsha, referring to her older sisters. "They would take feces and spread it all over my body. They would make me smear it on myself. They made me eat it."

I felt my heart break. Tears streamed down my cheeks. For a moment—a long moment—I just sat beside this deeply wounded woman, holding her, rocking gently back and forth. I could not fathom how human beings could treat another human being like that, especially a child. It was beyond my comprehension.

The thinking part of me began to search for explanations. Marsha was from North Carolina. That kind of thing seemed to suggest poverty to me. Rural? Urban? These were questions I could not ask, because regardless of why it happened or how it happened, Marsha needed help, and Jesus meant that afternoon to heal some aspect of that terrible nightmare. My job was simply to communicate his love.

"I sense that the Lord wants to give you a bath," I told Marsha, suggesting a way we might enter into healing prayer through the imagination. She smiled and thought the idea was wonderful. We both agreed that the two-year-old in her needed touching. Normally I would have pictured a scene in her family's bathroom, but that place must have been repulsive to her. In fact, any house or any bathroom in her real memory would have been too confining and not clean enough for what needed to happen. So we imagined a scene in nature: a lush green pasture with a blue sky and lovely lake.

Marsha smiled as she pictured herself being carried as a little two-year-old in Jesus' warm Shepherd's arm, across the meadow toward the lake. This "inner child" healing was a lot of fun because Marsha was so perfectly in sync with what the Lord wanted to do. Sometimes people have trouble imagining Jesus in the scene and I need to be somewhat directive in suggesting the sequence of events, but Marsha seemed to know exactly how the scene would unfold.

"Jesus is holding you in his arms," I said. "I don't really know what you're wearing."

"I'm not wearing clothes," she said. "I'm naked."

"Oh, you're beautiful," I said, now visualizing her as a cute little bare-bottomed girl. "You have beautiful clear skin, pink and pudgy."

"Are we there yet?" Marsha wanted to know. She was anxious to get in the water.

I laughed. "Yes, we're there. Jesus is wading into the water with you. You are cradled in his arms, looking up at him, and he swishes you back and forth gently through the water. Can you see Jesus looking down at you?"

"Yes," said Marsha. "His eyes are so loving. He looks like I imagine a daddy would look if he were looking down at his little girl. I didn't have a dad, but I think that is what it would be like."

"He takes great delight in you, Marsha. He loves your soft brown hair, your tiny toes. You have such a sweet smile. I see sunbeams shooting from your eyes."

"Yes," said Marsha, "I see them." Then she wanted to know if Jesus brought soap.

"Yes," I said. "He has a big bar of white soap in his hand. He's running it over your tummy and you're shaking with laughter. It tickles. He is working up a good lather, washing your legs and arms, behind your ears, even the cracks between your toes. You are squeaky clean all over. I see the soapsuds dissipating and floating away on the surface of the lake. Jesus throws the bar of soap over his shoulder, and it lands on the shore."

Then I saw Jesus put his hands on Marsha's waist; she was facing him. He bounced her up and down in the water playfully.

"That's wonderful," said Marsha, "but I want to be clean inside too. I still have a stench on my breath." She wrinkled her nose as if repulsed.

Marsha told me that when she was twenty-seven she had tried to commit suicide. The only thing that had saved her was drinking a bottle of Joy dishwashing soap after she had taken an overdose of pills and alcohol. She paused and looked at me with searching eyes. "I think I was trying to make myself clean inside."

The word *pneuma* came to my mind. Wind. Breath. Words used to describe the Holy Spirit in the Bible. We went back to the picture of Jesus bouncing little two-year-old Marsha up and down in the water. I told Marsha to open her mouth wide and take big gulps of air as she bounced up and down. "Feel the freshness, the mintiness, the cleanness of that air as it flows through your body. Let every muscle, every tissue, every cell breathe it in."

Then Jesus kissed little Marsha on the lips. He walked out of the lake and back across the meadow with her, whispering these words: "I know the plans I have for you . . . plans to prosper you and not to harm you, plans to give you hope and a future" (Jer 29:11).

And then, as if by some incredible orchestration of events (which it was), Mike Flynn asked for everybody's attention. We were to end individual ministry and sing together this song:

Lord, you are more precious than silver.

Lord, you are more costly than gold.

Lord, you are more beautiful than diamonds

And nothing I desire compares with you.

Marsha and I were standing now. As we sang together, Marsha clung to me, resting her head on my breast like a child nuzzling her mother. She was so relaxed and full of joy, soft and affectionate. All of the starkness had gone out of her hard appearance.

Mike told us to make the song more personal by substituting our own names, and I was able to sing this as a lullaby from Jesus to Marsha:

Marsha, you are more precious than silver.

Marsha, you are more costly than gold.

Marsha, you are more beautiful than diamonds

And nothing I desire compares with you.

It was a deeply moving moment for me. During the months leading up to Urbana, the Lord had been impressing upon me the vast expansiveness of his love: "Have you journeyed to the springs of the sea or walked in the recesses of the deep?" (Job 38:16). But when I experienced God's love for Marsha that day, it was as if all I knew of the vast, vast ocean of love suddenly shrank to a single drop of water in the palm of my hand.

I thought, *If only I can love my husband, my kids, people I meet with that kind of love, I will have within my heart a reservoir of love so vast that it can completely swallow up any hurt, any sin, and wash it over with a deep, renewing power.*

The session was soon over, and the crowd began to move out toward the doors. "The lake, the meadow, everything you pictured was exactly right," Marsha told me. "How did you know?" Of course I *didn't* know, but I believe powerful prayers of intercession during the conference really did double and triple the anointing so that Jesus was able to perform very deep healings in a remarkably short time. My ministry time with Marsha had lasted only about fifteen or twenty minutes.

Marsha asked for my name and address. "I want you to write me and tell me this actually happened," she told me. "This is so unbelievable. I can't believe it really happened." She had a little money in a long-distance telephone fund and wanted to know if she could call me.

Marsha's story is not over. With the Lord's help, she will receive appropriate counseling and be enfolded in the embrace of a warm body of believers who will love her back to wholeness. It will be a long road, but I believe she has the courage to keep going, and it was clear to me that afternoon that she is very sensitive to the Spirit and gifted to serve the Lord of Love.

How did prayer at Urbana affect Marsha's spiritual life? "This is a more intimate experience of prayer than I have ever had. I will pray differently. Praise more. I feel more freed up. And now I know that I can have a Father who will never abandon me."

From Marsha, December 30, 1990

Mike Flynn had asked the Holy Spirit to come. We were standing quietly, seven to eight hundred men and women at Urbana 90. We were instructed not to pray, but rather to wait.

While I stood there blank for a little while, the Holy Spirit seized my heart as if saving it from a great fire—an emergency, if you will. I had already prayed earlier in thanksgiving to the Lord for guiding me to the forgiveness seminar the day before. I had been praying this day about the seminar that was called "Holiness and Sexual Healing." I had to speak with the Holy Spirit that day to ask him to give me strength to go. I knew it as yet another act of the Holy Spirit's amazing grace which was guiding me that way. It was clearly his will that I attend this workshop (*I* most assuredly had *not* planned to attend). I was committed to going.

I found myself suffering from migraine headache symptoms; I felt really sick to my stomach, and the left side of my head was throbbing. I skipped the plenary session in order to prepare myself, with the generous aid of the Holy Spirit, to face yet again the monsters that could raise their heads at this seminar. I rebuked Satan by telling him to buzz off, but the pain increased. I was feeling less and less close to Christ Jesus as the torment continued. I kept going anyway. I walked through the ice and snow, falling a few times, but got back up and trudged on alone down the street with the help of the Lord.

I got to the seminar an hour early to ensure that I would be able to get in. No one was there yet. I took some more medication to shrink the blood vessels that were screaming in my pulsating head.

Determined to let God's will be done, I sat in the large theater in the dark. I began to pray. *Please, Holy Spirit, come to free me from the bonds of the past— incest that began at the age of two and was repeated over and over until I was raped at seventeen.*

While I had had five years of counseling, I still had a very emotional response to the words *childhood sexual abuse*. Thinking I was healed, I had terminated therapy approximately one year before.

Being a new child of Jesus, I had never really talked to him in prayer about my horrific experiences of humiliation and degradation at the hands of my mother. Only the day before had I prayed for forgiveness of her and others who had sexually abused me. Only yesterday had I begged God to forgive me for bearing any violent feelings toward those people. What follows is an account of the Holy Spirit's visit to me today, the day of the workshop.

As I stood there in the theater waiting for the Holy Spirit to move me, he came. Not quietly, gently or with trepidation as if I were fragile, but with a vengeance. As I said before, he seized my heart as if rescuing me from Satan's sabotage.

He said, "I can and will heal you," over and over—again, not in quiet tones but as a loud, very specific pronouncement. I realized then that my headache was gone. I am not sure when it left really, but by the time the Holy Spirit rescued me, it had disappeared.

I stood passively listening to this strong, powerful, nongender voice. I couldn't imagine how he would do it, but I knew he was dead serious. I didn't believe him. I was scared and peaceful simultaneously.

(I had asked the Holy Spirit earlier in the day to reveal to me what "normal" sexuality was/meant. I had asked him to make me whole if that were his will.)

Someone tapped me on the shoulder and asked me to pray to Jesus. I was weeping and sobbing. I was still very frightened. I was an open wound, but I knew not why. Secretly, though I asked for completeness, I never really believed he would come to me personally and let me know he had received my message. I didn't think he could really love such a filthy and vile person as I. My childhood sexual abuse had included a ritual my mother had performed with some friends and my sister. They used to make me strip down to my waist, and they would defecate and urinate on me, making me ingest their waste. I thought surely our most holy God cannot love someone as nasty as this. I was defiled. I couldn't recall whenever it was that I was truly innocent.

The first prayer minister to speak to me did most of the appealing to the Holy Spirit. She said that I didn't really believe that Jesus Christ, Lord of the Universe, could love *all* of me. (How could she know what I scarcely knew myself? How could she name the essence of the chasm between Jesus Christ and me before I had really admitted it to myself or the Holy Spirit?) She promised me that God could and did love all of me. (How could that be? I still doubted.) Further, the Holy Spirit told her to hold me, that I didn't think I was lovable. She assured me again that God certainly did.

We spoke and she prayed for quite a while, and then she left. I remained seated in the aisle and wept. She wasn't aware of why I felt so unworthy of his love.

Next came a blessed woman (Betsy Lee) who asked me what was going on. The Holy Spirit was still insistent that he/she would and could heal me: "I can and will heal you." By this time I was thoroughly spent and didn't put up much of a fight. His grand, tender hands were holding my heart as we began to pray.

The first thing out of Betsy's mouth was these words: "The Holy Spirit can and will heal you." I couldn't believe she used the same words the Holy Spirit had used! She too hugged me, and I felt the love of both her and the Holy Spirit engulfing me with a love that was steadfast and real. My anguish was deep, but I saw with my own eyes that Betsy mirrored my suffering while she enveloped me in her arms. It was as if the Holy Spirit were using her arms to reach me.

She was so sure Christ Jesus would mend the broken pieces, I began to believe it. I could see. I could see with my own eyes the possibility. Betsy and the Holy Spirit together began the process of repair.

I told her everything that was on my heart, disbelief, fear of being too polluted and sullied for God to love. I told her the details of the ugliness of parts of my defilement. I told her how I still felt befouled and that I needed to become clean.

Again, the most astonishing thing happened. We took a trip in our imaginations, guided by Betsy, to a field with a tremendous pond in it. I was two years old, and Jesus brought me there with great love in his face and in his whole body. He washed me in the water and we played there. I didn't exactly see him as a father, since I have no frame of reference for that, but I did see him as a man who loved me with great joy, and not a single sense of sexuality from him or me. We were indeed satisfied there—splashing and bouncing in the sparkling, still water.

As we finished the scene, I realized that I felt cleansed on the outside, but my insides were left rotting. I was so full of poison I felt as if surely he could see it. Betsy then took some time to come up with an idea for how we could purify my insides. I basked in the light of Jesus' gaze as he admired me in an uncomplicated, simple way, seeming to rejoice in the innocence of the moment. I started to feel warm.

Very carefully Betsy instructed me that the Holy Spirit and breath were somehow similar. I'm not sure whether they mean the same thing, or one word is derived from the other, or just how she said it. But the idea was given to her to suggest that Jesus blow the breath of the Holy Spirit inside me to purge my insides. This was a revolutionary idea! I was still imagining that I would have to ingest bottles of liquid soap to wash out the slime. Slowly but briefly (because we were running out of time), I imagined Jesus blowing into my mouth the cleansing, polishing breath of the Holy Spirit.

The seminar had to end at the time, and I was completely exhausted. I felt that I had lost fifty to sixty pounds the day before in the forgiveness seminar, but today I felt as if I were just a breath. I was no longer I. I was something gauzy, ephemeral, spiritlike, not of the flesh.

I am not sure how long that sense lasted, but Satan grabbed me sometime later with all the symptoms of a full-blown migraine. I was consumed with pain in a way that was clearly trying to block out the reality of the afternoon. I kept on rebuking the enemy. Others prayed for me. My bunkmate was praying quietly over me when I was awakened by her loud whisper. When I sat up, it turned out she was saying "in Jesus' name." Satan had attacked her while she interceded for me. He knocked her to the floor. She got a chair and rebuked the enemy, not giving up.

My torment lasted into the night, but I knew Satan could never take the experience away from me. He knew it too. By morning he had given up, and all signs of the migraine were gone. It was easy to tell it was from the enemy because when I have a "real" headache, it takes roughly three days to recover. I was much stronger the next day than I had ever felt before.

Praise the living God.

Praise the loving Lord Jesus.

Praise the power of the joy of the Holy Spirit.

Notes

Chapter 1: What Is the Ministry of Inner Healing?
[1]Here and throughout this book, names and other identifying features have been changed in order to safeguard the privacy of people we have prayed for.
[2]In the event of very severe abuse, such as enforced participation in ritualistic sacrifice, there are other ways that children are impacted, as in the development of alternative personalities. Even in such cases, however, the *degree* of trauma seems to depend upon the response of the child to the abuse.

Chapter 2: How We Became Involved in Inner Healing
[1]This story is told in chapter five of Michael Flynn, *Holy Vulnerability* (Old Tappan, N.J.: Chosen Books, 1990), p. 66.

Chapter 3: Theological Underpinnings
[1]See J. Wilkinson, "Healing," in *New Dictionary of Theology,* ed. Sinclair B. Ferguson, David F. Wright and J. I. Packer (Downers Grove, Ill.: InterVarsity Press, 1988), p. 287.
[2]Michael Green, *I Believe in Satan's Downfall* (Grand Rapids, Mich.: Eerdmans, 1981), p. 208.
[3]See chap. 4 on sowing and reaping in John Sandford and Paula Sandford, *Transformation of the Inner Man* (Tulsa, Okla.: Victory House, 1982), especially p. 75.
[4]David Seamands, *Healing for Damaged Emotions* (Wheaton, Ill.: Victor Books, 1981), p. 21.
[5]Ken Blue, *Authority to Heal* (Downers Grove, Ill.: InterVarsity Press, 1987), pp. 69-78.

Chapter 4: Using the Bible in Inner Healing

[1]Sandford and Sandford, *Transformation of the Inner Man*, p. 242.
[2]Thanks to Laurie Niewoehner, friend and partner in ministry at Faith United Presbyterian Church, for ideas in this section and other sections of this chapter.
[3]See chapters seven, eight, eleven and twelve for extended discussion of methods of praying for others.

Chapter 5: Jesus' Healing Authority

[1]Reframing is an effective intervention developed by cognitive behavior therapists.
[2]See the treatment of "omnipotency" in children in chapter nine, "Psychological Factors."
[3]Norman Grubb, *Touching the Invisible* (Fort Washington, Penn.: Christian Literature Crusade, 1978), p. 33.
[4]A full treatment of this dynamic can be found in Sandford and Sandford, *Transformation of the Inner Man,* chap. 14, p. 237 and following.
[5]For an extremely useful treatment of the function of worldview, we recommend *Christianity with Power* by Charles H. Kraft of Fuller Theological Seminary; Vine Books, 1989. The subtitle is instructive: *Your Worldview and Your Experience of the Supernatural.*
[6]See Thorleif Boman, *Hebrew Thought Compared with Greek* (New York: W. W. Norton, 1960), p. 123 and following.

Chapter 7: Praying for Oneself

[1]From George MacDonald, *Unspoken Sermons,* series 1 (Eureka, Calif.: J. Joseph Flynn Rare Books/Sunrise Books, 1989), pp. 106-7.
[2]The word translated "condemn" in 1 John 3:20 and "condemnation" in Romans 8:1 is *kataginosko,* which literally means "to know something against." There is thus a play on words in these verses: "If our heart *knows* something against us, God is greater than our heart and *knows* all things." "Therefore there is no *knowing* against those who are in Christ Jesus."
[3]Hebrews 4:12; Isaiah 55:11; Jeremiah 23:29; Matthew 24:35.
[4]From Flynn, *Holy Vulnerability,* pp. 61-63.
[5]If you have doubts about using the imagination in concert with God, you may want to skip ahead and read that section in chapter ten, "Frequent Mistakes."

Chapter 8: Praying for Others

[1]See the section on forgiveness in chapter six.
[2]See the sections on Jesus' lordship in chapter five and intimacy with God in

chapter six.

[3]Unconfessed sin in a generational line gives the enemy "permission" to tempt and oppress succeeding generations. We reap from the sins of others "to the third and fourth generation" (Ex 34:7) and beyond. See section on "Our Problem" in chapter three. Also see chapter twelve on spiritual warfare.

[4]Chapter four contains a more detailed examination of Psalm 139 as a framework for praying inner healing.

Chapter 9: Psychological Factors

[1]This quotation is taken from Earle Fox's newsletter, *Emmaus News* 1 (February 1992). (Available from P.O. Box 21, Ambridge, PA 15003.)

[2]Table 2 was first published in Flynn, *Holy Vulnerability,* p. 50.

[3]This is not to suggest that psychologists' only valid function is to unearth data for inner healing. My point is to show that a psychologist and an inner healer can have a cooperative relationship.

Chapter 10: Frequent Mistakes

[1]The KJV translates this word in Matthew as "see" or "seeing" fifty-five times, as "know" or "knowing" twenty-five times, as "perceive" and "tell" once each.

Chapter 11: Working with the Spirit

[1]Think, for example, of the Spirit coming on Samson when he defeated a lion (Judg 14:6), on Saul when he prophesied (1 Sam 10:10) and upon Azariah who inspired Asa's reform (2 Chron 15:1).

[2]John 3:27; 5:19-20, 30; 7:16, 18, 28; 8:28-29, 38; 9:33; 12:49; 13:20; 14:10, 24, 31.

Chapter 12: Spiritual Warfare

[1]Mark Bubeck, *The Adversary* (Chicago: Moody Press, 1975), and *Overcoming the Adversary* (Chicago: Moody Press, 1984). Michael Green, *I Believe in Satan's Downfall* (Grand Rapids, Mich.: Eerdmans, 1981). Charles Kraft, *Defeating Dark Angels* (Ann Arbor, Mich.: Servant/Vine, 1992). Francis MacNutt, *Healing* (Notre Dame, Ind.: Ave Maria, 1974). Peter Wagner and Douglas Pennoyer, eds., *Wrestling with Dark Angels* (Ventura, Calif.: Regal Books, 1990). Thomas White, *The Believer's Guide to Spiritual Warfare* (Ann Arbor, Mich.: Servant/Vine, 1990).

[2]See chapter four, "Using the Bible in Inner Healing," for a longer review of the biblical understanding of Satan's work.

[3]There are many important questions raised by spiritual warfare and deliverance

ministry. It is beyond the scope of this book to deal with all of these questions.
Our desire is to illustrate warfare as it relates to inner healing prayer ministry.
For example, we assume in our discussion, and hope the reader is in agreement, that Christians can be oppressed and attacked by demonic spirits
(though *not* possessed). For discussion regarding this and other issues we
refer you to White, *Believer's Guide to Spiritual Warfare,* chap. 11, "What
Everyone Seems to Want to Know About Spiritual Warfare" (pp. 147-63), or
Charles Kraft, *Defeating Dark Angels,* chap. 11, "Questions and Answers" (pp.
215-38).
[4]See, for example, MacNutt, *Healing,* pp. 208ff.
[5]Ibid., pp. 161-66; table 4 adapted from p. 167.
[6]Kraft, *Defeating Dark Angels,* p. 43.
[7]Ibid., p. 132.
[8]Ibid.; see especially chap. 6, "Demonic Attachment and Strength," pp. 119-38.
[9]Ibid., p. 197.
[10]Bubeck, *The Adversary,* includes an excellent chapter on "tools for warfare"
(pp. 135-53) with several excellent prayers for daily warfare.

Chapter 13: Wider Dimensions of Inner Healing
[1]A note regarding procedure: If the gathering has not been explicitly promoted
as an inner healing event, you will need to declare your intention to pray for
inner healing, ask the group's permission and explain enough about inner
healing to enable them to collaborate with it before you pray.
[2]A chapter in Flynn, *Holy Vulnerability,* explores this topic at greater length.
[3]John Dawson, "Seventh Time Around: Breaking Through a City's Invisible
Barriers to the Gospel," in *Engaging the Enemy,* ed. C. Peter Wagner (Ventura,
Calif.: Regal Books, 1991), pp. 135-42.

Appendix: Marsha's Story
[1]Betsy's account is copyright 1991 by Betsy Lee; reprinted with permission. The
account written by "Marsha" is also used by permission of the author.